Build GenAI Agents with OpenAI + vLLM

Develop portable AI agents in Python with structured outputs, tool calling, OpenAI Agents SDK, vLLM, model switching, CLI, API, and Docker deployment

Stew Wao

Copyright © 2026 by GitforGits

Published by: GitforGits

www.gitforgits.com

Printed in India

First Printing: February 2026

ISBN: 978-93-49174-24-5

Cover Design by: Kitten Publishing

Disclaimer:

This book, including all its text, diagrams, and illustrations, is an original work developed for educational and informational purposes. The content is not affiliated with, endorsed by, or sponsored by OpenAI or any other company, brand, or entity referenced within. All brand names, product names, and trademarks mentioned are the property of their respective owners and are used in a descriptive, educational context only. Every effort has been made to ensure that no copyrighted or trademarked material has been copied or misused in this book. All diagrams and illustrations that are not original have been used with proper attribution and credit to their respective sources.

If you believe that any content in this book infringes upon the copyright or trademark, please contact us immediately at support@gitforgits.com. Upon notification, corrective action will be taken promptly.

Prologue

There's no way I'd forget the moment I started getting the idea for this book. There was no conference or formal research session. It happened while I was messing around late at night with a small Python script that called a language model. My name's Stew Wao, and like a lot of developers working with AI systems, my mind was totally blown by the sudden rise of AI agents. Everywhere I looked, people were building assistants, automations, and workflows powered by large language models. But every experiment I tried felt a bit unstable. It looks like changing the model version broke something. We had to rewrite half of the code when we switched providers. So, when we tried a new SDK, that meant learning a whole new interface. At first, it was just out of curiosity, but then it hit me like, "Oh, this isn't just about building agents, it's about building them in a way that can keep up with constant change."

After looking at a bunch of early projects, I noticed a trend. The developers were tying their application logic directly to whichever framework or SDK they started with. That approach worked well for a demo, but it rarely lasted. The models changed, the providers evolved, and new tools appeared almost every month. As I kept playing around, I started to care less about the models themselves and more about the architecture around them. I was curious about what would happen if we designed agents the same way we design reliable software systems. The way we did that was by separating business logic from infrastructure, defining clear interfaces, and keeping core behavior independent from the tools that execute it. And during these explorations, I noticed something encouraging. When the architecture was simple and disciplined, the surrounding complexity became manageable. If the tools follow strict contracts, an agent could call them without causing any problems. It's easier to work with model responses when they're shaped into structured outputs instead of free-form text. The change from a hosted model to a local inference engine like vLLM was just a configuration change, not a total rewrite. The SDK could even become interchangeable if the application logic lived in a stable core module and the SDK itself was treated merely as a runtime adapter. The more I experimented with these patterns, the more I realized that building durable AI agents was less about choosing the right framework and more about choosing the right design principles.

This book came from those experiments and observations. It doesn't try to predict the future of artificial intelligence or promise instant automation. Instead, it focuses on practical engineering habits that make agent systems easier to maintain as the ecosystem evolves. We'll build an agent step-by-step, starting with a small loop that accepts input and produces structured output. As we go, we'll add tools, validation, model switching, runtime adapters, and packaging techniques that'll let the agent move from a simple script to a reusable application.

While you're going through the chapters, you'll probably notice that the examples are intentionally simple. They're easier to reason about, test, and adapt when the tech around them changes. Ultimately, you'll be able to build an AI agent and structure it in a way that allows it to keep up as models, SDKs, and deployment environments evolve.

Content

Preface

AI agents are getting easier to build, but the surrounding ecosystem of models, SDKs, and frameworks is changing quickly. A lot of agent apps get tricky to maintain since they depend too much on a certain provider, library, or deployment setup. This book looks at a practical alternative, which is to make AI agents whose main logic doesn't change while models, SDKs, and runtimes can be changed around it. It's not about using complicated frameworks. Rather, this book shows you simple architectural patterns that let you set up an agent application so that tools, schemas, prompts, and business logic can stay separate from the runtime layer.

For starters, it'll be a simple loop with agents, and we'll gradually build on that with tools that make things deterministic, outputs in a structured JSON format, and schema validation. It'll teach skills, like switching between models through configuration, running the same agent with hosted models or local inference using vLLM, and isolating SDK-specific integrations behind small adapter layers. Later, we will focus on packaging and deployment, in which we will convert the agent into a command-line tool, expose it through a minimal HTTP API, and package the application using Docker. Ultimately, the book puts the project together as a reusable starter template that can be used as a basis for future agent-based applications.

Instead of talking about shortcuts or automation, this book focuses on practical development patterns for building maintainable AI agents. Basically, this book is perfect for Python developers, software engineers, and AI practitioners who want a step-by-step process for designing agents that can adapt as the surrounding ecosystem changes.

In this book you will learn to:

- Build **GenAI agents** using simple agent loop that accepts prompts, calls tools, and returns structured AI responses.
- Use **structured JSON outputs and Pydantic schemas** to make AI agent responses reliable and safe for automation.
- Design **AI tools as deterministic Python functions** so agents can call calculators, summarizers, and utilities predictably.
- Create **portable AI agents** by separating business logic from LLM and model APIs.
- Implement a **model gateway pattern** to switch between OpenAI models, local LLMs, or other providers via configuration.
- Run the same agent with **OpenAI models or local LLM inference using vLLM**.
- Prevent SDK lock-in by isolating **AI SDK integrations behind runtime adapters**.
- Use **LLM regression prompts and schema validation** for better stability of AI Agents during switching the models.
- Package **AI agent as CLI tool and HTTP API** for real applications and integrations.
- Deploy AI agents with **Docker containers and environment variable**.

GitforGits

Prerequisites

If you're interested in building GenAI agents with OpenAI + vLLM, this is a clear, hands-on guide to creating portable AI agents using Python. It's geared toward Python developers, software engineers, and AI practitioners who want a methodical approach to design agents that stay adaptable to the future AI innovation and developments.

Codes Usage

Are you in need of some helpful code examples to assist you in the programming and documentation? Look no further! Our book offers a wealth of supplemental material, including code examples and exercises.

Not only is this book here to aid you in getting the job done, but you have our permission to use the example code in the programs and documentation. However, please note that if you are reproducing a significant portion of the code, we do require you to contact us for permission.

But don't worry, using several chunks of code from this book in the program or answering a question by citing our book and quoting example code does not require permission. But if you do choose to give credit, an attribution typically includes the title, author, publisher, and ISBN. For example, "Build GenAI Agents with OpenAI + vLLM by Stew Wao".

If you are unsure whether the intended use of the code examples falls under fair use or the permissions outlined above, please do not hesitate to reach out to us at support@gitforgits.com.

We are happy to assist and clarify any concerns.

Acknowledgement

I owe a tremendous debt of gratitude to GitforGits, for their unflagging enthusiasm and wise counsel throughout the entire process of writing this book. Their knowledge and careful editing helped make sure the piece was useful for people of all reading levels and comprehension skills. In addition, I'd like to thank everyone involved in the publishing process for their efforts in making this book a reality. Their efforts, from copyediting to advertising, made the project what it is today.

Finally, I'd like to express my gratitude to everyone who has shown me unconditional love and encouragement throughout my life. Their support was crucial to the completion of this book. I appreciate the help with this endeavour and the continued interest in my career.

Acknowledgement

Chapter 1: Shipping GenAI Agent in Minutes

Overview

In this chapter, we will begin with building a portable GenAI agent from zero. We will start by establishing a clear definition of what an agent means in this work, focusing on the loop pattern where an agent repeatedly accepts input, determines whether a tool call is needed, and then either performs the tool action or produces a final output. This looping structure is essential because it mirrors how real GenAI agents interact with tools and models, giving us a conceptual anchor for all subsequent development. We will also implement a minimal version of this loop in Python to help us internalize how agent logic works step by step, and we will keep the example small so we can run and explore it interactively.

After defining the agent loop, we will set up a clean project structure with a source folder and a script folder, and we will build an entry script that runs our agent logic. We will also show how to centralize configuration such as model name, endpoint, and API key into a single config module that our code reads from environment variables. We will run our first prompt against the agent to verify that everything is wired correctly. To make our development experience smooth and transparent, we will introduce basic logging that records model selections, request identifiers, and final outputs. With this, we are going to have a working, interactive agent template that we can extend safely in further chapters.

Getting Started with AI Agents

The concept of an "agent" actually started way before the modern generative models popped up. The old-school definition of AI is that it's something that perceives its world, makes a decision, and then acts to change that world. In the old days, a human engineer would write rules that matched certain patterns and tell the system what to do in each case. Those early definitions still fit perfectly with the outer loop we'll build here. ***What's changed recently is how decisions are made.*** Today's generative models can reason in language and suggest actions like tool calls or final responses, instead of having hardcoded rules. Even though things have changed, the outer shape is still a loop because the pattern is the same. We still receive input, decide what to do, act on that decision, and then deliver output.

From a high-level perspective, humans and software agents seem pretty similar since they both take in information and use it to take action. A person uses their senses, values, memory, and goals to decide what to do next. Whereas, an agent just uses the data we give it and the logic we build. This difference makes us say exactly what our agent can and cannot do. We humans can figure out meaning from context or intuition. Our agent can't do that unless we code it or the model inside provides it. Throughout this book, we'll keep that difference clear so our architecture remains understandable and portable as we swap frameworks and models later.

Currently, models like those from OpenAI, Anthropic, DeepSeek, Google or local servers such as vLLM can suggest actions in the form of structured outputs. Sometimes they suggest that a tool should be called with specific arguments. The code then runs that tool and sends the results back to the model. This interaction is exactly what defines the agent shape.

In this opening topic, we will build a ***tiny version of that loop*** so we can run it and understand it completely before we bring in production SDKs or model backends. The loop we build now will stay recognizable in later chapters even when we swap models or switch the underlying engine.

Agent Definition

For our work, we will use a precise definition:

An agent is a loop that takes input, calls tools when needed, and returns a final response.

This definition is quite simple, actionable, and gives us a clear structure of an AI agent with the following components:

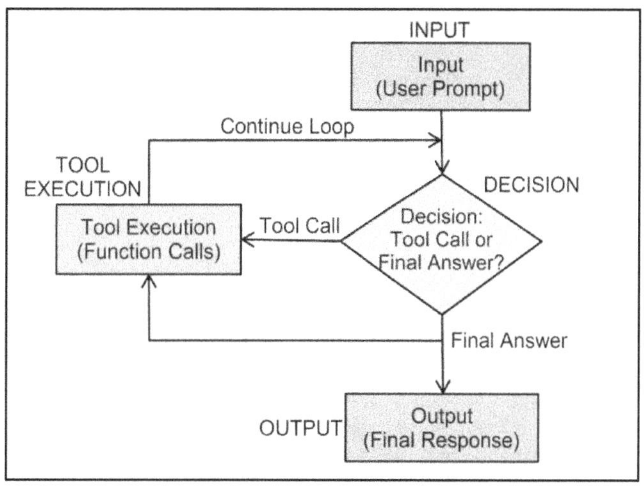

Fig 1.1 AI Agent Structure

1. ***Input*** is a prompt we type in the terminal.
2. ***Decision*** is a step that chooses either a tool call request or a final answer.
3. ***Tool Execution*** are function that does some real work. And,
4. ***Output*** which is a final message printed to the console.

We will build a small runnable version of the above definition so that we can grow our agent into more capable forms while keeping the core loop constant.

Deterministic Tool

Our first step is to ***define a simple tool the agent can use***. In later chapters we will add many tools including web search, vector databases, and file systems. For now, we will begin with ***a simple calculator*** that evaluates arithmetic expressions.

So, let us start. We will first create a Python file named **`agent_loop.py`** and type the following code:

```
# agent_loop.py
import re
def calc(expression: str) -> str:
    """
    A very simple calculator tool that evaluates arithmetic
expressions.
    It accepts only digits and arithmetic operators to keep it
safe.
    """
    if not re.fullmatch(r"[0-9+\-*/ ().]+",
expression.strip()):
        return "Tool error: unsupported characters."
    try:
        result = eval(expression, {"__builtins__": {}}, {})
        return str(result)
    except Exception as exc:
        return f"Tool error: {exc}"
```

This function takes a string with an expression and returns a string result.

This small function matters because it shows us how to design a tool that is both simple and safe. It has a strict input contract, predictable output, and error handling that keeps things controlled. This clarity is the pattern we will continue to follow for all tools in the further book.

Decision Step

In AI agents, the model generally decides whether to call a tool or generate a final answer. Until we bring models into the loop, we need a placeholder that mimics this behavior. We will write a simple function that checks for a pattern like **`calculate: <expression>`** and returns either a tool call request or a direct answer otherwise.

So here, we need to add the following code in the same file immediately below the **`calc`** function:

```
from dataclasses import dataclass
from typing import Dict, Any, Optional
```

```
@dataclass
class ToolCall:
    name: str
    args: Dict[str, Any]
def decide(user_prompt: str) -> tuple[Optional[ToolCall],
Optional[str]]:
    """
    Decide whether to call a tool based on the prompt.
    If we see a calculation pattern, we request the calculator
tool.
    Otherwise we prepare a direct final response.
    """
    match = re.search(r"calculate\s*:\s*(.+)$",
user_prompt.strip(), re.IGNORECASE)
    if match:
        return ToolCall(name="calc", args={"expression":
match.group(1).strip()}), None
    return None, f"Final response: {user_prompt}"
```

This function returns a tuple with either a **ToolCall** object or a final text. Our loop will interpret the first element as a tool call request and the second as a final response. It's a simple way to keep the interface consistent for both outcomes.

Agent Loop

We now connect our tool and our decision function in a loop that reads input from the terminal and processes prompts one line at a time. This loop will repeat until we type **quit**.

Following is what we will then add to **agent_loop.py**:

```
TOOLS = {"calc": calc}
def run_agent() -> None:
    print("Type a prompt. Type 'quit' to exit.")
    while True:
        user_prompt = input("> ").strip()
```

```
        if user_prompt.lower() == "quit":
            print("Stopping.")
            return
        tool_request, final_text = decide(user_prompt)
        if tool_request:
            tool_fn = TOOLS.get(tool_request.name)
            if tool_fn is None:
                print(f"Tool error: unknown tool
'{tool_request.name}'")
                continue
            tool_output = tool_fn(**tool_request.args)
            print(f"Tool result: {tool_output}")
            print("Final response: Tool completed.")
            continue
        print(final_text)
if __name__ == "__main__":
    run_agent()
```

Here, this loop does exactly what our definition of an agent requires:

- It reads input from us.
- It calls the decision function to choose a tool or final response.
- It runs the tool if requested and prints results.
- It prints a final response and waits for the next prompt.

We can then run the script with:

```
python agent_loop.py
```

When we type:

```
> calculate: 8 * (3 + 2)
```

you will see:

```
Tool result: 40
```

```
Final response: Tool completed.
```

And if we type something that is not a calculation:

```
> hello agent
```

you will see:

```
Final response: hello agent
```

Overall, this tiny working loop gives us a good ignition. We can confidently extend it with models, structured outputs, model switching, and SDK layers later without breaking the core idea. Our loop will stay intact even as we add complexity because that definition of an agent never changes.

Creating Repo Layout

When a new developer or a collaborator opens a codebase, the first thing they see is the folder hierarchy. A messy layout will create cognitive overhead even for the original creator. And, this overhead scales badly with project size, especially for applications like GenAI agents where many components such as tools, gateways, and integrations will cohabit the same codebase as the project evolves.

Hence, my personal recommendation is to organize application code into clearly named directories. And, we should avoid scattering many loose scripts at the root. Also, the tests shall be hold separately in a dedicated folder to isolate testing concerns from core implementation. For our work, we will begin with a minimal layout as it does not demand elaborate layers.

Initial Layout

We will begin with a structure that is minimal and practical too:

- We will keep our code in a dedicated source directory so it is not mixed with configuration files or documentation.
- We will place our script files inside the source directory so our imports and Python execution paths stay clear and predictable.
- We will create a configuration area if needed so we can place environment variables, model settings, and provider details in one place. And,
- We will reserve space for other top-level concerns such as tests and documentation, even if they are empty for now, because this prepares the project for growth.

Folder Structure

We will start with a top-level folder for our entire project. For the sake of teaching, we will name it **genai_agents**. Within it, we will add a source folder named **src** and a script folder named **scripts**. In the later chapters, we will add additional folders such as tools, configs, and tests.

So, for now, we will create the project root directory and then the minimal subfolders:

```
genai_agents/
├── src/
└── scripts/
```

The **src** folder will hold all reusable modules that define our agent logic. And, the **scripts** folder will hold entry scripts that bind our core logic to commands that run from the terminal.

Adding Python file

We need to place the runnable script that starts our agent. And, we will place that script under the **scripts** folder. By doing so, it isolates the entry point of our application so that later we can add different entry points (for example CLI tools, API servers, or tests) without cluttering the source directory.

So, we will create **run_agent.py** inside **scripts** folder. And, the content of it should be simple as below:

```
# scripts/run_agent.py
from src.agent_loop import run_agent
if __name__ == "__main__":
   run_agent()
```

In the above script, we are simply importing the **run_agent** function from our main logic and calling it. However, this will happen only after we migrate it into the **src** folder, which we will see in the next step.

Initializing Source Directory

Now, we move our **agent_loop.py** code into **src** directory so that our core logic lives inside a named space for our project. We will place that file inside **src**. The new layout now looks like:

```
genai_agents/
├── src/
│   └── agent_loop.py
└── scripts/
    └── run_agent.py
```

This structure is clear and extensible. The later chapters might add additional modules such as tools, gateway modules, configuration loaders, and test files.

Running Script

Now that we have the entry script and the agent loop placed under controlled folders, we can verify it with one run command:

```
python scripts/run_agent.py
```

Since the source code lives under **`src`**, the Python can easily locate the imported **`agent_loop`** module and execute **`run_agent()`** as expected.

As we proceed through this book, we will expand this layout thoughtfully. We will add **`configs`** for model and SDK settings, **`tools`** for additional capabilities, and **`tests`** for automated checks.

Single Config Module for Model Settings

A common pattern I have noticed for managing sensitive settings such as API keys is, to avoid hardcoding them directly in source code. Instead, we should try to load them from environment variables. This keeps sensitive information out of the repository and makes it easier to control access without risk of accidental exposure.

In addition, it also helps with validation of settings at application startup to catch missing or malformed values before the agent runs. It thereby improves reliability and prevents subtle failures at runtime.

Your key learning in this topic is, that we should be able to create a ***configuration module*** that:

- Loads the model's name, endpoint URL, and API key from environment variables in a single place.
- Provides defaults where reasonable.

- Does not require rewriting the agent logic when we swap models later. And,
- Can be extended in further development to include additional settings such as timeout, provider type, or gateway options.

Designing Config Module

At first, we will create a new file under **src** directory called **config.py**. This module will be responsible for loading and validating the settings that the agent and its model gateway do require.

So, the first step is to determine configuration values we need. I have outlined some of them as below:

- **MODEL_NAME**

This setting defines the model we are going to use, such as a hosted OpenAI model string or the default model for local vLLM.

- **API_BASE_URL**

This holds the base URL of the model provider API. We will start with a default of the hosted endpoint and can override it in environment variables for local vLLM.

- **API_KEY**

This will be loaded from an environment variable. We will use a standard name such as **OPENAI_API_KEY** so that other tools and SDKs can share it without conflicting.

Implementing Config Module

Next, we will create **src/config.py** with logic for loading environment variables. For this, we will use the built-in **os** module to get variables.

Following is the content we must place inside the **src/config.py**:

```
# src/config.py
import os
# Load the model name from environment
MODEL_NAME = os.environ.get("MODEL_NAME", "default-model")
# Load API base URL
API_BASE_URL = os.environ.get(
    "API_BASE_URL",
    "https://api.openai.com/v1"
)
```

```
# Load the API key
API_KEY = os.environ.get("OPENAI_API_KEY")
# Validate essential settings
if not API_KEY:
   raise RuntimeError(
       "Configuration error: OPENAI_API_KEY is not set in the environment"
   )
```

At this point, our project structure looks like:

```
genai_agents/
├── src/
│   ├── agent_loop.py
│   └── config.py
└── scripts/
    └── run_agent.py
```

Using Config Module in Agent Code

Now that we have a central config module, we will update parts of our agent code that need model settings so they import values from **src/config.py**. For this, we will first open **src/agent_loop.py** and add the import for **config** near the top of the file.

For now, we do not need **MODEL_NAME**, **API_BASE_URL**, or **API_KEY** in the agent loop, but we can still have them imported for the next chapters:

```
from src.config import MODEL_NAME, API_BASE_URL, API_KEY
```

If we run the agent now, we will see no change in behavior, but this import confirms that the config module is executing and validating environment values. If we forget to set the API key environment variable, the config module will raise an error early, such that we do not experience a silent failure later.

Setting Environment Variables

We will now define the environment variables in a **.env** file at the project root, with following script:

```
MODEL_NAME=gpt-4.1-turbo
API_BASE_URL=https://api.openai.com/v1
OPENAI_API_KEY=sk-yourkeyhere
```

One most important I want to share here, is that we must add this file to **.gitignore** so that this file never gets committed to version control. It helps us to protect our sensitive key values:

```
# .gitignore
.env
```

When we start the shell session for local work, we can load these variables into environment:

```
export OPENAI_API_KEY="sk-yourkeyhere"
export MODEL_NAME="gpt-4.1-turbo"
export API_BASE_URL="https://api.openai.com/v1"
```

And, we can confirm if they are available successfully:

```
echo $OPENAI_API_KEY
echo $MODEL_NAME
echo $API_BASE_URL
```

The environment variables in such a way allows us to switch models and endpoints with configuration only. When we later run against a local vLLM server, we just have to simply override the **API_BASE_URL** and the **MODEL_NAME**, without modifying application code.

The key benefit of this config module, is to focus on agent behaviour and model interactions later without worrying about how settings are passed around.

Running Prompt through Agent

So far, our project has:

- A clean structure with **src** for core logic and **scripts** for entry points.
- A central config module that loads model settings and secrets from environment

variables.

- The agent loop logic placed under **`src/agent_loop.py`**.
- A simple script in **`scripts/run_agent.py`** that starts the agent.

Before we run the agent and type our first prompt, it is important for us to confirm that the wiring between our environment settings and code is correct. We will test that next.

Setting up Environment Variables

Before we execute the agent script, we must ensure that the environment variables required by our config module are present. The environment variables are loaded by Linux/MacOS before the Python process starts.

So, in shell, we type the following:

```
export OPENAI_API_KEY="sk-your-secret-key"
export MODEL_NAME="gpt-4.1-turbo"
export API_BASE_URL="https://api.openai.com/v1"
```

These values will be visible to Python via **`os.environ`** which behaves like a dictionary mapping variable names to string values.

While we do, I recommend that we avoid storing sensitive data like API keys directly in code. The environment variables provide a clear separation between code and configuration. This pattern makes the code portable and secure across local machines, containers, and production environments. It also allows us to switch models or API endpoints without rewriting application logic, exactly as we want for later chapters.

Running Agent Script

After this, we are ready to run the agent. We run the agent from the project root with:

```
python scripts/run_agent.py
```

Once the script starts, we should see a prompt in the console asking for our input. You just need to provide a simple prompt.

So, at the prompt, we can type:

`> calculate: 3 + 5`

The agent loop inspects this input using the decision function we wrote earlier. Since the prompt matches our calculation pattern, the loop invokes the **`calc`** tool, and then the tool evaluates the arithmetic expression, returning a string result. The agent prints both the tool result and the final response:

```
Tool result: 8
Final response: Tool completed.
```

If instead of the arithmetic, we type something that does not match the calculation pattern, for example:

> hello agent

Then, the agent will respond immediately with a direct final response using the fallback logic in the decision function:

```
Final response: hello agent
```

This behaviour shows us that the loop, decision step, and tool calling mechanism are working together correctly in the context of our project layout and config setup.

Confirming Environment Variables and Config Wiring

To confirm that our environment variables are correctly loaded and used by the config module, we can modify our project temporarily to print out config values at startup. However, instead of printing them, I advice you to guard this check, because the secret values like the **OPENAI_API_KEY** will be disclosed.

So here, we can add a small snippet in the entry script right before the agent loop begins:

```
from src.config import MODEL_NAME, API_BASE_URL, API_KEY
print(f"Config check: MODEL_NAME set to {MODEL_NAME}")
print(f"Config check: API_BASE_URL is {API_BASE_URL}")
if not API_KEY:
   print("Config error: API_KEY appears missing")
else:
   print("Config check: API_KEY loaded")
```

Once we run the above script, it will print our configuration values (except the secret) and confirm that the config module is retrieving values properly from the environment.

For now, we have verified that our first runnable script works and that our configuration wiring is solid. And, it is really a major milestone for us, in the early evolution of our agent project.

Adding logger

When we think about how our agent operates, we want more than just a final answer printed to the console. We want to ***see what happened under the hood***. The great thing about logging is that it gives us a continuous view of program execution, not just at the moment of a crash but across normal runs. The logs that are good tell a story about what the agent did, what model it selected, what input it received, and what output it produced. Every log entry is like a little story about what happened.

The Python's built-in **logging** module provides us to configure log levels, formatting, and handlers so that our outputs are both human-readable and machine-parsable when needed.

Configuring Logger for Agent

We will add the logging setup at the top of **src/agent_loop.py**. Below is the code to place at the top of **src/agent_loop.py**, before any function definitions:

```
import logging
logging.basicConfig(
    level=logging.INFO,
    format="%(asctime)s [%(levelname)s] %(message)s"
)
logger = logging.getLogger(__name__)
```

After this configuration, all the logs at or above **INFO** level are going to be displayed. It also includes the timestamp and level indicator for better clarity and visibility into key steps without noise.

Logging Selected Model

In our project, the model's name and base URL from **src/config.py** are very important because they determine which inference backend we will later use. Even though our initial agent loop does not call a model yet, the printing of this configuration at startup gives us confirmation that configuration is reads correctly and consistently.

So here, we will add a log entry right after we import config values in **src/agent_loop.py**:

```
from src.config import MODEL_NAME, API_BASE_URL
logger.info(f"Using model: {MODEL_NAME} at {API_BASE_URL}")
```

This step is actually a sanity check that helps while debugging the configuration issues.

Generating Run Identifier

To make logs more traceable, it is often useful to include a request identifier or run session ID. This identifier helps us tie log entries across steps that belong to the same prompt execution. Even when logs appear interleaved in multi-session environments, a unique identifier lets us filter and group related logs. Although a simple timestamp can act as an identifier for now, adopting a unique request ID pattern helps later when agent runs become concurrent or distributed.

So here, we will generate a simple request ID before processing each prompt in our loop:

```
import uuid
while True:
    user_prompt = input("> ").strip()
    if user_prompt.lower() == "quit":
        logger.info("Received quit command. Stopping agent.")
        break
    request_id = uuid.uuid4().hex
    logger.info(f"Request {request_id} received:
{user_prompt}")
```

In the above, we are using the Python standard **uuid** module to generate a unique hex string per prompt. We'll log this at the start of each request to get a unique anchor for the whole lifecycle of that prompt's processing. We've found this approach lightweight and works well.

Logging Final Output

After the agent chooses a tool, call, or final response, it's extremely important to record the outcome. You can use this info to figure out how the input was understood and what action the agent took. Our plan is to use the existing decision logic and add log entries at key points:

1. ***Decision step outcome*** in which whether a tool will be called or a final response is produced.
2. ***Tool execution result*** logs what the tool returned. And,
3. ***Final agent response*** wherein we log what the agent prints back to the user.

Below is how we update parts of the loop to include these logs:

```
tool_request, final_text = decide(user_prompt)
if tool_request:
    logger.info(f"Request {request_id}: Tool call requested for
{tool_request.name}")
```

```
    tool_fn = TOOLS.get(tool_request.name)
    if tool_fn is None:
        logger.error(f"Request {request_id}: Unknown tool
'{tool_request.name}'")
        print(f"Tool error: unknown tool
'{tool_request.name}'")
        continue
    tool_output = tool_fn(**tool_request.args)
    logger.info(f"Request {request_id}: Tool
'{tool_request.name}' returned {tool_output}")
    logger.info(f"Request {request_id}: Final response
generated")
    print(f"Tool result: {tool_output}")
    print("Final response: Tool completed.")
    continue
logger.info(f"Request {request_id}: Final response:
{final_text}")
print(final_text)
```

After the above additions, our each prompt will produce a sequence of log entries. And, it will clearly showcase:

- Which request was received.
- Whether a tool was called.
- What the result of the tool call was. And,
- What the final agent output was.

And, such logs reflect the sequence of significant actions with contextual information tied to that request ID, which is very helpful for debugging.

Reading Logs

So just to try it out, we can simply run **`python scripts/run_agent.py`**, and then we can see log entries:

```
2026-03-01 14:22:35 [INFO] Using model: gpt-4.1-turbo at
https://api.openai.com/v1
```

```
2026-03-01 14:22:40 [INFO] Request af7c9f24… received:
calculate: 3+5

2026-03-01 14:22:40 [INFO] Request af7c9f24…: Tool call
requested for calc

2026-03-01 14:22:40 [INFO] Request af7c9f24…: Tool 'calc'
returned 8

2026-03-01 14:22:40 [INFO] Request af7c9f24…: Final response
generated
```

If we could see in detail, each log entry provides a timestamp and the message level, and we see exactly how the agent handled the prompt step by step.

Summary

To quickly summarize our learnings, we saw how an agent continually takes an input, decides whether to call a tool, executes the tool if needed, and returns a final response. We built the smallest runnable form of this loop in Python so that we could run it immediately and see how it worked, reinforcing the pattern of input, decision, tool, and output that modern agents use.

We then organized the project with a simple folder layout, created an entry script to invoke the agent, and introduced a centralized config module to handle model settings and environment variables. We validated the environment variables being loaded correctly, and ran a first prompt to confirm that everything was wired correctly. Finally, we added basic logging so that each prompt run showed which model was selected, a unique request ID, and the final output, giving us early visibility into agent behavior. This chapter did give us a complete, though a short baseline from which we could grow our agent system with confidence.

Chapter 2: Building Agent Workflows

Overview

In this chapter, we will deepen our agent's capabilities by teaching it to call practical Python tools. We will start with tools as function contracts, examining why it is important to specify what each service built into our agent expects and guarantees. We will then implement a simple deterministic calculator tool with explicit validation and clear error messages, followed by a text summarizer that turns unstructured paragraphs into bullet points and action items.

After building individual tools, we then explore tool registry pattern that centralizes registration, lookup, and management of available tools. And lastly, we will integrate predictable error handling into the agent loop so that tool failures are recognized as clear signals, logged appropriately, and handled gracefully without causing crashes or unintended loops. This chapter is meant to prepare us to build strong agent workflows that can reliably perform actions and handle failure cases.

Function Contracts

A ***function contract*** describes ***obligations and guarantees*** of a piece of code before it is executed and after it returns. In our everyday life, a contract is a clear agreement about what one party must provide and what it can expect in return. In programming, that same idea becomes a mutual promise between the function itself and its caller. A contract specifies what inputs are required, what outputs are guaranteed, and what conditions must hold true both before and after execution. This approach, often called ***design by contract***, as it helps developers to write clearer interfaces and enables early detection of failures.

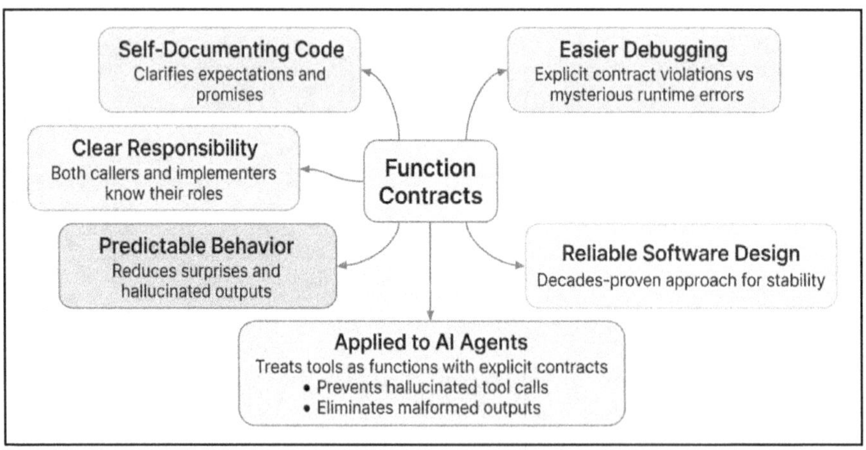

Fig 2.1 Benefits of Function Contracts

There are a few benefits to formalizing function contracts. It helps clarify what a function expects and what it promises to return, making code more self-documenting. Plus, contracts make it easier to figure out what's going wrong, since failures in the input usually lead to clear contract violations instead of those sneaky runtime errors tucked away in complex call stacks. It's all about knowing who's responsible when the function's contract is clear. This clarity is why contract programming has been part of reliable software design for decades, and why we'll ***treat tools in our agent as functions with explicit contracts***. It'll help keep our agent behavior predictable and reduce surprises, like hallucinated tool calls or malformed outputs.

Why Function Contracts for AI Agents?

In the context of AI agents, tools are external capabilities the agent uses to extend its reasoning beyond language output. A tool might perform a web search, calculate a value, handle a database query, or trigger an API call. When a model requests a tool call, it needs to know exactly ***what shape that tool expects*** and ***what form of result it will return***. If these expectations are vague, the model might generate incorrect arguments or misinterpret the tool's output. That ambiguity becomes especially problematic when the model proposes incorrect arguments or the tool fails silently without clear error signals. We want to reduce such unpredictable behavior to keep agent actions reliable and observable.

In addition, a well-defined contract makes a tool's responsibilities clear, its interface easy to call, and its return values predictable. When a tool's contract is explicit, the agent's decision logic becomes easier to reason about, and debugging becomes simpler because we can trace exactly whether the model provided valid arguments and whether the tool honored them. A tool with explicit input requirements and output guarantees also curtails what we call ***hallucinations*** (these are situations where the model produces outputs that are plausible in language but make no logical sense in the context of the tool). A strict contract becomes a checkpoint that a tool call must satisfy before the agent executes it. The model may say "***call this tool with these arguments***," but if the arguments do not satisfy the contract, we can catch that early and handle the error cleanly rather than letting the system go off into unintended behavior. This ultimately reduces the unpredictability and enforces consistency across agent runs.

Python Functions with Contracts

We will now apply this idea practically. We will define a tool with a strict contract. In our existing project, we will add a new file under **`src/tools`** folder. We will begin with a simple text summarizer tool, then show how its contract enforces clarity around inputs and outputs. Our tool will accept a single string input and return a string output. For example, it will return a summary of the input if the input is non-empty, and it returns a clear error message if not.

So, we will begin now. We will first create a file **`text_tools.py`** inside **`src/tools`** and then we will define the following function:

```
# src/tools/text_tools.py
from typing import Protocol
class TextSummarizerContract(Protocol):
```

```
    text: str
def summarize_text(text: str) -> str:
    """
    Summarize the given text.
    Preconditions:
    - text must be a non-empty string.
    Postconditions:
    - Returns a summary string that is shorter than the input
text
      and contains key points extracted from the text.
    """
    if not isinstance(text, str):
        return "Tool error: input must be a string."
    if not text.strip():
        return "Tool error: text is empty."
    # Simple split-and-take logic for demonstration
    words = text.split()
    half = len(words) // 2
    summary = " ".join(words[:half])
    return summary
```

In the above, we have defined a protocol interface for clarity, but the heart of this tool is the function **summarize_text**. The docstring carefully states:

- ***Preconditions*** of what must be true before the function is called, such as **text** being a non-empty string. And,
- ***Postconditions*** of what the function promises after execution, such as returning a shorter summary.

Now, from our agent loop, when we want to call this tool, we know exactly what we expect and what we will get back. This stops an invalid invocation early and keeps our agent from executing unintended side effects.

Overcoming Hallucinations

The term ***hallucination*** in AI refers to a model producing text that is plausible but factually incorrect, or syntactically valid but logically unsound. The models can hallucinate largely because they predict based on patterns rather than strict validation constraints. If an agent loop blindly accepts every model proposal as valid, these hallucinations can propagate into real tool calls and cause unexpected outcomes.

So here, we can have strict rules about contracts for tools, and they will act like ***guardrails*** for this process. When a model proposes arguments to a tool, those arguments have to satisfy the contract before execution. If they don't, the contract checks will reject them, and we can choose how the agent should handle such rejections. This gives us control over the agent's behavior rather than letting it wander into unintended execution paths.

For example, if the model suggests:

```
call summarize_text with text = 12345
```

Then, our function's precondition immediately fails because **`text`** is not a string. The contract directs us to return an explicit error:

```
Tool error: input must be a string.
```

This is far better than letting the wrong type go into some opaque model operation or cause a runtime exception later. With contract-driven design, we can define recovery strategies such as prompting the model to regenerate arguments in the correct format, logging an error, asking the user for clarification, or falling back to a default behavior. This clarity is particularly important in GenAI systems where the language model's outputs can be fluid. With strict contracts, we ensure that only valid, predictable tool interactions occur.

Building Deterministic Tool

In our previous topic, we learned that tools in an AI agent should behave like functions with well-defined input and output contracts. A deterministic tool is one that produces the same output every time for a given input and has clear, predictable behavior without side effects. In contrast to models that can generate different outputs on repeated runs, deterministic tools act like mathematical functions, in which the result is always identical, if given the same arguments.

So here, if we give an agent a calculator tool with strict validation rules, it can ensure that when the agent needs to compute numbers it uses a source of truth for arithmetic rather than guessing.

Defining Calculator Tool Contract

Before we write any code, we will quickly identify what this calculator tool should do, like:

1. Accept a clear arithmetic expression as input.

2. Validate that the expression contains only allowed characters (digits and arithmetic operators). And,
3. Return a result string representing the computed value or a clean error message if input validation fails or computation is unsafe.

Implementing Calculator Tool

We will now implement it. We will first create a file **calculator_tool.py**. In this file, we will define the **calc** function that serves as our calculator. Because we are writing with contracts in mind, we will validate inputs before attempting any computation.

Following is the complete code for **src/tools/calculator_tool.py**, which we can simply copy it:

```
# src/tools/calculator_tool.py
import re
def calc(expression: str) -> str:
   """
   Calculator tool that evaluates a simple arithmetic 
expression.
   Preconditions:
   - expression must be a string
   - expression must contain only digits, parentheses, 
whitespace,
     and arithmetic operators + - * /
   Postconditions:
   - returns the evaluated numeric result as a string
   - or returns a clear error message if validation fails
   """
   if not isinstance(expression, str):
       return "Tool error: expression must be a string."
   cleaned = expression.strip()
   if not cleaned:
       return "Tool error: expression is empty."
```

```
    # Validate allowed characters for safety
    if not re.fullmatch(r"[0-9+\-*/ ().]+", cleaned):
        return "Tool error: expression contains unsupported characters."
    try:
        # Evaluate in a restricted environment
        value = eval(cleaned, {"__builtins__": {}}, {})
        return str(value)
    except Exception as exc:
        return f"Tool error: {exc}"
```

Now, let me explain what we did in the above code:

- We used a regular expression to allow only digits, spaces, parentheses, and the four basic arithmetic operators.
- We explicitly returned error messages when input conditions were not met. And,
- We used a restricted **eval** call with no built-ins to reduce unintended behavior.

This tool does not produce side effects or raise uncaught exceptions for most malformed inputs.

Updating Agent to Use Calculator Tool

Next, we will now integrate the tool into our agent loop so our agent can actually use it. For this, we will just update the **TOOLS** dictionary in the agent loop to include this new calculator function:

```
from src.tools.calculator_tool import calc
TOOLS = {
    "calc": calc,
}
```

This sort of updation or wiring allows our decision logic to call the correct tool implementation. If the agent loop detects a calculator request, it will fetch the tool from the dictionary and execute it with validated input.

Tool Calling with Prompts

Next, we will now try a prompt in the agent loop:

```
> calculate: 2 + 3 * 4
```

The decision step will detect the calculator request, call the **`calc`** tool with the expression **`"2 + 3 * 4"`**, and the tool will return **`"14"`** because it evaluates the arithmetic correctly. The loop will then print:

```
Tool result: 14

Final response: Tool completed.
```

If we try a malformed expression:

```
> calculate: 2 + three
```

The regular expression validation prevents unsupported text and returns a clear error:

```
Tool result: Tool error: expression contains unsupported characters.

Final response: Tool completed.
```

In the above, in case, if the agent receives a malformed request, then the tool responds with a predictable error rather than causing a runtime exception or an undefined result.

Without a deterministic tool, the agent relies on model-generated calculations. And, the models do make mistakes in computation. Hence, with a dedicated calculator to our agent, and with a strict contract, we remove that uncertainty and provide a canonical source of truth for arithmetic tasks. Instead of guessing, the agent calls a tool that is designed to compute exactly and reliably.

Summarizer Tool for Workflows

For our agent project, one of our tools is a summarizer. It's a deterministic function with a clear contract that takes a text input and returns a structured summary. Even though these language models can summarize stuff, using a tool with specific behavior lets us control what we expect and integrate it easily into our agent framework. When you're dealing with a lot of information, having a clear structure like bullet points and action items can make it easier for other applications to understand and use the summary. This is useful in situations like processing meeting notes, analyzing reports, and setting up automation triggers, where people need easy-to-understand summaries.

Contract Design

Before writing the code, we will, at first, design the contract for our summarizer tool. As we learned in the previous topic, a good tool contract specifies what it expects and what it guarantees.

Hence, for our text summarizer, the contract will be:

- ***Input*** which is going to be a string of arbitrary text, possibly multi-paragraph and verbose.
- ***Preconditions*** can be like the input must be a non-empty string with at least one sentence.
- ***Output*** will be a structured summary, with bullet points and optionally action items if discernible. And,
- ***Postconditions*** will be that, the output string is non-empty, with each summary bullet and action item clearly separated.

Implementing Text Summarizer

To implement the summarizer tool, here too we will first create a new file **`text_tools.py`** under **`src/tools`**. The following is a simple heuristic summarizer that transforms paragraphs into bullet points and identifies sentences containing keywords like "should", "need to", or "task" as action items:

```
# src/tools/text_tools.py
from typing import List
def summarize_text(text: str) -> str:
   """
   Summarize the given text into bullet points and action
items.
   Preconditions:
   - text must be a non-empty string
   Postconditions:
   - Returns a structured summary with bullets and action
items
   """
   if not isinstance(text, str):
       return "Tool error: input must be a string."
   stripped = text.strip()
   if not stripped:
       return "Tool error: text is empty."
```

```
    lines: List[str] = []
    action_items: List[str] = []
    # Split on sentences using simple period separation
    sentences = [s.strip() for s in stripped.replace("\n", "
").split(".") if s.strip()]
    for sentence in sentences:
        # Identify potential action items based on rudimentary
keyword patterns
        lowered = sentence.lower()
        if "should" in lowered or "need to" in lowered or
"must" in lowered:
            action_items.append(f"- [ACTION]
{sentence.strip()}")
        else:
            lines.append(f"- {sentence.strip()}")
    summary_parts: List[str] = []
    if lines:
        summary_parts.append("Summary:")
        summary_parts.extend(lines)
    if action_items:
        summary_parts.append("Action Items:")
        summary_parts.extend(action_items)
    # Join parts with newlines
    return "\n".join(summary_parts)
```

This implementation does not cover advanced NLP techniques, and instead uses simple sentence splitting and keyword lookup.

Integrating Summarizer Tool into Agent

After this, we will integrate it into our agent's tools dictionary so the agent can invoke it based on prompts. To do this, we will update the agent loop script with following:

```
from src.tools.text_tools import summarize_text
```

```
TOOLS = {
    "calc": calc,
    "summarize_text": summarize_text,
}
```

This registration allows our agent loop to call **`summarize_text`** when the decision step identifies a summarization task. For now, our simple decision logic does not yet detect summarization prompts automatically by keyword, but we will update that logic shortly.

Extending Decision Logic

If we want the agent to be able to use this tool based on a prompt, we'll need to tweak the decision function in the agent loop. There's a prompt pattern that indicates a summarization request.

For example:

```
summarize: <long text>
```

We then modify the **`decide`** function to recognize this pattern and return a **`ToolCall`**:

```
match_sum = re.search(r"summarize\s*:\s*(.+)$",
user_prompt.strip(), re.IGNORECASE)
if match_sum:
    return ToolCall(name="summarize_text", args={"text":
match_sum.group(1).strip()}), None
```

With this logic in place, when a user enters a summarization request, the agent will correctly route it to the **`summarize_text`** tool.

Running Summarization

Let us try out here. We simply run the agent and then we enter a prompt:

```
> summarize: Our team met yesterday to discuss the upcoming
release. We should finalize the report by Friday. The
documentation needs to be updated. There will be a conference
next week.
```

The decision step will detect the summarization intent and produce a tool call. The summarizer runs and returns the structured summary as shown before.

To sum up, we've extended our agent's practical capabilities by implementing the summarizer as a Python function with a strict contract and predictable output. And with such a way, we've maintained a stable core architecture that future changes won't break.

Create Tool Registry

With more developments, the agent will start to depend on many practical tools that perform different functions. If we simply hard-code every function into the agent loop, the code quickly becomes cluttered and hard to maintain.

So here, a registry pattern helps us collect tools in one place and control what tools are available at runtime. That way, we can add or remove tools without rewriting core logic in the agent loop. The basic idea is that each tool registers itself with a central registry that maps a tool's name to a function handler. Later, when the agent wants to call a specific tool by name, it looks it up in the registry. And trust me, this pattern is quite a standard in many of the software designs.

Designing Tool Registry

The first step is to create a central module that maintains a dictionary of tool names to function handlers. We will call this module **tool_registry.py** and place it under our **src** folder in the project. The registry will expose functions to register tools, retrieve tools by name, and optionally list available tools. In addition to this, we may also want the registry to support dynamic enable/disable of tools at runtime.

Implementing Tool Registry

As usual, we will first create a file **src/tool_registry.py**, and in this file, we will maintain a global dictionary of tools and provide functions for registering, retrieving, enabling, and disabling them.

Given below is how we implement it:

```
# src/tool_registry.py
from typing import Callable, Dict
# Central dictionary mapping tool names to function handlers
_registered_tools: Dict[str, Callable[..., str]] = {}
def register_tool(name: str, handler: Callable[..., str]) ->
None:
    """
    Register a tool handler with a given name.
    Args:
```

```
        name: The unique string identifier for the tool.
        handler: The callable function that implements the
tool.
    """
    if name in _registered_tools:
        raise ValueError(f"Tool '{name}' is already
registered.")
    _registered_tools[name] = handler
def get_tool(name: str) -> Callable[..., str]:
    """
    Retrieve a registered tool by its name.
    Raises:
        KeyError: If no tool with that name exists.
    """
    if name not in _registered_tools:
        raise KeyError(f"Tool '{name}' is not registered.")
    return _registered_tools[name]
def list_tools() -> Dict[str, Callable[..., str]]:
    """
    Return the dictionary of all registered tools.
    """
    return _registered_tools
def disable_tool(name: str) -> None:
    """
    Remove a tool from the registry so it cannot be called.
    """
    _registered_tools.pop(name, None)
```

This above simple registry module provides us with:

- Tools that are registered only once with a unique name.

- Tools that can be looked up by name and executed by the agent.
- We can list all registered tools for introspection or debugging. And,
- We can also disable tools by removing them from the registry.

Registering Tools in the Registry

With the registry module in place, we can now register both, the calculator and the summarizer too. We will use **`register_tool`** so each tool adds itself to the central dictionary. The code for registering tools would typically live in a setup or initialization section of our agent application like in a new file or at the top of **`src/agent_loop.py`**:

```
from src.tool_registry import register_tool
from src.tools.calculator_tool import calc
from src.tools.text_tools import summarize_text
register_tool("calc", calc)
register_tool("summarize_text", summarize_text)
```

After this, the registry will now contain both tools, and we do not need to maintain a hard-coded **`TOOLS`** dictionary inside the agent loop itself.

Modifying Agent Loop for Registry

To keep things more current, we then have to update the agent loop, so it can consult the tool registry instead of a hard-coded dictionary. Below is the updated section of the loop where we talk about tools:

```
from src.tool_registry import get_tool
tool_request, final_text = decide(user_prompt)
if tool_request:
   try:
       tool_fn = get_tool(tool_request.name)
   except KeyError:
       print(f"Tool error: unknown tool
'{tool_request.name}'")
       continue
   tool_output = tool_fn(**tool_request.args)
```

```
print(f"Tool result: {tool_output}")
print("Final response: Tool completed.")
continue
```

In the above, we replaced direct dictionary lookup with a call to **`get_tool`**. If a tool is disabled or unregistered, **`get_tool`** will raise a **`KeyError`**, and we print a clear error message.

This whole about registry improves maintainability, reduces duplication, and supports scalable growth of agent capabilities over time. You can think of the registry as a simple plugin framework, wherein the tools register themselves, the agent calls them by name, and new tools can be added later without modifying the core logic.

Predictable Error Handling

In Python, errors that occur at runtime are called ***exceptions***, and they normally cause a program to stop unless those exceptions are anticipated and handled proactively using **`try`** and **`except`** blocks.

For our agent, when a tool returns an error signal, the agent should treat that as an explicit outcome rather than interpret it as part of a normal successful response. This clear separation of success and failure allows the agent loop to remain stable over time, avoids misleading outputs, and gives us a surface where we can program fallback logic or corrective actions without silent failures.

Defining Standard Error Signals for Tools

To begin with, we shall first determine what constitutes an error signal from a tool. A standard and simple pattern is:

- A tool ***returns a string that starts with a clear prefix*** such as **`"Tool error:"`** when something goes wrong.
- That error string should inhabit a well-defined space so the agent logic can detect it without ambiguity. And,
- The agent loop can then decide how to handle an error case: log it, notify the user, re-prompt the model for corrected arguments, or skip further execution instead of looping indefinitely.

Unlike letting an unhandled exception propagate up and crash the entire process, this standardized error signal allows the agent reason about failure explicitly and take fallback measures.

Building Tools with Predictable Error Signals

We have already seen this pattern in our calculator and summarizer tools. For example, in our calculator tool implementation form the previous topic, the validation logic returns strings beginning with **"Tool error:"** for unsupported characters, empty input, or invalid types. That means we can test for that exact prefix in the agent loop and handle it accordingly, rather than treating it as normal output.

I am giving you a simple code for the calculator tool's contract, just in case we wish to refer:

```
if not isinstance(expression, str):
    return "Tool error: expression must be a string."
```

From the above, we do not want uncaught exceptions bubbling out of a function, rather we are expecting every outcome either a valid correct result or a clear error message that can be interpreted.

And, the same pattern exists in our summarizer tool:

```
if not stripped:
    return "Tool error: text is empty."
```

Use this consistent prefix pattern for errors to give us a reliable way to detect faults, no matter which tool reports them.

Detect Error Responses

Next, we will also try to update the agent loop. It will support to handle cases explicitly. Instead of printing error strings as if they were results, the loop can examine tool outputs and handle the failures with fallback logic.

The given below is the updated snippet for tool execution inside the agent loop:

```
try:
    tool_output = tool_fn(**tool_request.args)
except Exception as exc:
    logger.error(f"Request {request_id}: Tool
'{tool_request.name}' raised exception: {exc}")
    print(f"Tool error: internal exception in
'{tool_request.name}'")
    print("Final response: Agent could not complete tool
call.")
    continue
```

```
# Check if the tool returned an error signal
if isinstance(tool_output, str) and
tool_output.startswith("Tool error:"):
    logger.warning(f"Request {request_id}: Tool
'{tool_request.name}' reported error: {tool_output}")
    print(tool_output)
    print("Final response: Agent could not complete tool
call.")
    # Fallback or next action logic could go here,
    # for now we just stop processing this prompt.
    continue
```

From the above script:

1. We wrap the actual tool call in a **`try`** block to catch unforeseen runtime exceptions. If an unexpected exception does occur (for example, due to an invalid internal state), we catch it, log it, and provide a generic error response instead of allowing the program to crash.
2. Once the tool returns, we check if the result is a string that starts with our defined error prefix. If so, we treat it as a failure case and can handle it separately from normal output. And,
3. We also print a clear error message and a fallback final response rather than looping further to prevent agent from entering undefined or repetitive behavior in response to error outcomes.

This whole thing keeps the agent's behavior predictable because it no longer continues blindly with error results. Instead, it recognizes errors as first-class signals with explicit meaning. For example, let us assume that the agent encounters a calculator request but the input is malformed as shown below:

`> calculate: 2 + three`

Now here, instead of crashing or producing a confusing output, the tool returns:

```
Tool error: expression contains unsupported characters.
Our updated loop sees that this output starts with "Tool
error:", logs a warning, and prints:
Tool error: expression contains unsupported characters.
Final response: Agent could not complete tool call.
```

This response sequence gives context both to human readers and to possible automation monitoring systems. The agent loop stops handling this prompt and waits for the next, avoiding repeated loops based on a bad tool call.

This whole pattern reduces ambiguity and helps ensure that the agent's behavior remains understandable and stable even in the face of malformed inputs or unexpected tool failures.

Summary

To sum up the learnings, we upskilled to extend the basic agent loop with practical tools and a clear function contract. We built a simple calculator tool that validated arithmetic expressions and returned either computed results or clear error messages, and we added a text summarizer that transformed messy paragraphs into structured bullet points and action items.

Next, we explored central tool registry to manage available tools which includes to register, retrieve, list, and disable tools dynamically without cluttering the core agent loop. And lastly, we learned to add predictable tool error handling in the loop so that failures were signaled clearly using a consistent error prefix, caught with structured checks, and resulted in controlled fallback responses instead of silent crashes.

CHAPTER 3: RELIABLE AND STRUCTURED AGENT OUTPUT

Overview

The core agenda in this chapter is, to focus on making agent outputs reliable and predictable. And for this, we will adopt structured output formats, especially JSON, instead of relying on free-form text. We will begin by understanding why free-form language model responses are inherently brittle for automation and how structured outputs based on JSON schemas provide a clear contract between the model and our application logic. You will learn how schema-driven outputs eliminate ambiguity, reduce the need for fragile parsing code, and help build resilient systems that do not break when model behavior changes or when prompts are modified.

Next, we will introduce Pydantic, a Python library that lets us define structured output models with type validation, and we will teach how to implement a simple schema with fields like **`answer`**, **`steps`**, and **`confidence`**. We will learn to update the agent to instruct models to generate valid JSON that conforms to this schema, followed by Python code to validate responses and fail fast whenever the output does not adhere to expected types or structure. We will then show you to build a golden prompt regression test as a simple quality check that we can run whenever we switch models or revise prompts.

Structured Outputs

Free-Form Responses

Large language models are inherently excellent at producing rich conversational text. However, when an application expects information in a precise, machine-readable format, unstructured or ***free-form text*** becomes a liability. The free-form model outputs can vary dramatically in wording, formatting, punctuation, and structure from one generation to the next. A model might produce an answer that looks plausible to a human reader, but when software tries to parse that text into fields, lists, or values, unpredictable variations make robust automation difficult and error-prone. Without constraints, the free-form text often leads to brittle parsers, tangled regular expressions, or fragile post-processing scripts that break unpredictably when the model phrasing shifts. This mismatch between creative freedom of natural language the rigid expectations of software systems undermine reliability of automation built on raw model outputs.

On the other hand, when the text generation process is constrained, the use of structured formats creates a contract between what the model generates and what the consuming code expects. The shape and fields of the output have to follow predefined rules, which makes it possible to programmatically process the data without extensive parsing logic or error handling for unexpected variations. The way they do this is by using something called "structured outputs." These outputs are basically the foundation of reliable agent apps because they take creative model reasoning and turn it into data that's easy for other systems to understand and use.

Role of JSON Schema

A structured output is simply data that adheres to a specified format such as JSON, XML, or a custom schema. Among these, ***JSON schemas*** are one of the most common tools for defining data structure in software applications. A JSON schema acts as a blueprint that specifies what fields are required, what data types they must be, and what constraints apply to values. When a model produces output and that output is validated against a JSON schema, the result is a clear contract: yes, the output matches the expected shape, or no, it does not. That contract becomes incredibly valuable for application code because it eliminates the guesswork associated with textual responses. JSON schemas help ensure that critical fields are always present, always of the right type (for example, string, number, boolean, or list), and that the overall structure conforms to the expectations. This ability to enforce shape and type means the agent's output becomes ***machine-readable and predictable***, enabling downstream systems such as databases, APIs, or decision engines to consume the data directly without fragile parsing logic.

There is also some language model platforms now support structured output modes natively, where we can attach a JSON schema to a request and the model constrains its generation to match that schema. In those cases, the model itself produces output that can be validated immediately, reducing errors and eliminating many ad-hoc parsing steps. Such an approach makes integration with code much simpler because structured data can flow through APIs, be stored in databases, and be used in computations without qualms about format inconsistencies.

Structured JSON

The structured JSON outputs are all about ***application safety and operational stability***. It's like having a solid foundation for making decisions, updating states, and triggering events. Plus, it makes it easier to interact with other services without having to worry about malformed or unpredictable input. The structured outputs make it easy for developers to validate incoming data, thoroughly test agent behaviors-driven workflows, and build automated error handling based on schema violations rather than guesswork. If we build on structured data instead of free-form text, applications are less likely to crumble when models are retrained, updated, or switched to different providers. The way schemas make everything consistent means that even if the underlying reasoning changes, the output shape stays the same. This protects the business logic and integrations downstream from breaking.

If we use JSON schemas with structured outputs, we can take a language model's creativity and turn it into data that's easy for machines to understand and use. Instead of wrestling with unpredictable paragraph text, structured JSON lets applications work with a data contract that both humans and machines can trust.

Pydantic Output Model

So here, we are looking to define shape and type of the data so our code can rely on it without guessing. The ***Pydantic*** is a Python library that helps with just that. It lets us create ***models*** that describe the structure of expected data using type annotations. So, when we instantiate a Pydantic model, it ***validates*** the input values and ensures the resulting object matches the types we declared. If something does not conform, the Pydantic raises a clear validation error instead of letting bad data slip through silently. This behavior makes our code safer and easier to maintain especially when dealing with external inputs such as agent outputs, configuration files, or JSON APIs.

Also, the Pydantic models are like Python's **`@dataclass`**, but they include built-in validation, parsing, and serialization features that go beyond basic data storage. The Pydantic uses Python's type hints such as **`str`**, **`int`**, **`list`**, or even nested models to enforce correctness and consistency at runtime. When a Pydantic model is created, it ensures that each attribute complies with its declared type, and it may coerce some inputs (like converting a string to an integer) when safe to do so. Such combination of structure and validation makes this Pydantic an ideal choice for defining schemas for agent outputs.

Why Pydantic Output Model?

In the previous chapter, we saw free-form text is brittle when automation consumes it because natural language can vary unpredictably. In contrast, a Pydantic model lets us specify exactly what fields should be present and what type each field must have. When our agent returns a structured JSON payload and we validate it against a Pydantic model, we ensure that the output the agent generates meets our expectations ***before*** we use it in code. This prevents runtime errors caused by missing fields, wrong data types, or malformed data structures, and it gives us a reliable way to express a contract between model output and application logic. Because Pydantic raises explicit errors if validation fails, we can catch issues early and handle them gracefully. This helps us build agent apps that do not crumble when data arrives with unexpected shape or type.

Creating Pydantic Schema

So now, we will create a Pydantic model that represents the structured output we want our agent to produce. To make it simpler, we expect our agent to return three things:

- a human-readable answer string,
- a list of intermediate steps or reasoning traces, and
- a numerical score (for example between 0.0 and 1.0) indicating how confident the agent is about its result.

To begin, as usual we will create a new file **`src/output_schema.py`** and define the following:

```
from typing import List
from pydantic import BaseModel
class AgentOutput(BaseModel):
    answer: str
```

```
    steps: List[str]
    confidence: float
```

In the above code,

- **`answer: str`** tells Pydantic that the **`answer`** field must be text,
- **`steps: List[str]`** tells Pydantic that **`steps`** is a list of text items, and
- **`confidence: float`** tells Pydantic that **`confidence`** must be a floating-point number.

Agent Output with Pydantic Model

Now here, let us assume that we received the following agent output from some part of our system:

```
raw_agent_output = {
    "answer": "The result is 42",
    "steps": ["Received input", "Computed value"],
    "confidence": 0.87
}
```

Now in this, we will use the Pydantic model to validate and parse the output as shown below:

```
from src.output_schema import AgentOutput
validated = AgentOutput(**raw_agent_output)
print(validated.answer)         # "The result is 42"
print(validated.steps)          # ["Received input", "Computed
value"]
print(validated.confidence)     # 0.87
```

In the above, if any of the fields were missing or had the wrong type (for example, **`steps`** were given as a single string instead of a list), then the Pydantic would raise a **`ValidationError`** that includes clear information about which field failed to validate and why.

By wrapping raw agent outputs in a Pydantic model, we make a ***firm contract*** between the agent's output and our application's expectations. This helps us avoid fragile parsing logic and frees us from making brittle assumptions about the data. If a step is missing or the confidence score is malformed, Pydantic catches the mismatch before the data enters business logic, preventing silent failures.

In the next topic, we will learn to enforce this schema during actual model responses so that the agent produces output that conforms to this shape.

Schema Validation and Valid JSON

We have witnessed in the previous topics, that the prompt engineering techniques can coax a model toward producing JSON, but they do not ***guarantee*** that the output matches the exact schema we need without explicit enforcement. A model might still include extra prose, stray punctuation, or unexpected field names unless we instruct it carefully and validate the result afterwards.

So here, we will learn to tighten the agent's output contract so that whenever it produces a response, it ***must*** be valid JSON matching the Pydantic schema we defined in the previous section.

Prompt Strategy for valid JSON

To enforce structured output at the language model level, we give the model ***explicit instructions*** that describe exactly what JSON it must produce. These instructions should:

- Specify that the entire response must be valid JSON (no extra markdown, text, or commentary outside the JSON object).
- Include the exact keys and expected types as defined by our Pydantic schema (**`answer`**, **`steps`**, and **`confidence`**). And,
- Use phrasing that tells the model not to include any fields outside the schema and not to wrap the JSON in narrative text.

In the following, I am giving you a simple prompt template:

```
You must respond only in valid JSON with the following fields:
{
 "answer": "string",
 "steps": ["string", ...],
 "confidence": number
}
Do not include any additional text or explanation.
Please provide the JSON response for the following input...
```

In the above, the model knows the ***shape*** it needs to produce and knows that other text is not allowed. Now here, without such a strict framing, the model often returns JSON inside prose or includes extra elements, which breaks parsing logic and defeats the purpose of structured output.

Consequence of Loose Instructions

Consider the following attempt to get structured output using a loose instruction:

```
Summarize the following input and respond in a JSON format
with keys "answer", "steps", and "confidence".

Input: The sky is blue and the sun is bright today...
```

The model will produce prose with JSON embedded, such as:

```
Sure! Here is the summary:

{

 "answer": "The weather is clear.",

 "steps": ["The model read the input", "The model
summarized"],

 "confidence": 0.85

}
```

While this looks like JSON, the inclusion of non-JSON text before the object (such as "Sure! Here is the summary:") means it is ***not*** valid JSON according to strict programmatic parsing. Most JSON parsers will reject this response because it contains extra characters outside the JSON object. This happens because the instruction was not explicit enough that the ***entire response must be pure JSON with no additional text.*** This is a failure of the output contract, and we should tighten the contract so this does not occur in the first place.

Tightening Output Contract

So now, we have to make the instruction more precise and unambiguous. A tightened instruction might look like:

```
Respond only with a valid JSON object that contains exactly
the following keys: "answer", "steps", "confidence".

The value of "answer" must be a string. The value of "steps"
must be an array of strings.

The value of "confidence" must be a number.

Do not include any explanation or extra text outside the JSON
object.
```

```
Input:
<our agent prompt text here>
```

This above instruction removes complete ambiguity.

Validating and Parsing JSON Output

After the strict instructions, we will validate the returned JSON against our expected schema using our ***Pydantic model*** before using it in business logic. So here, when the structured output is correct, we can do:

```
validated = AgentOutput.parse_raw(model_response_text)
print(validated.answer)
```

If the output is invalid JSON or does not match required fields or types, the Pydantic raises a **`ValidationError`**, which we can catch and handle gracefully. This double layer of ***tight prompt instruction plus schema validation*** guarantees that only structured data enters our application logic.

This whole practice of forcing valid JSON plus schema validation is a great mechanism for building apps that consume agent outputs in production systems.

Validating Outputs and Fast Failing

The concept of failing fast is that, if something is wrong with the data, we stop execution immediately, report the error clearly, and do not proceed further with potentially unsafe assumptions. This practice aligns with a well-known engineering principle: "***detect problems early where they occur, not where they surface later.***"

So, when we enforce structured outputs from an agent, the next step is to ***validate those outputs before using them*** in code. When we validate early and ***fail fast*** on invalid data, we catch problems at the earliest possible moment, which greatly reduces debugging effort and development time. This practice is valuable as we change models, tweak prompts, or switch providers, because even small variations in model output can manifest as unexpected types or missing fields.

Validate Structured Output

Since we defined a **`Pydantic`** model in the previous topic (**`AgentOutput`** with fields **`answer`**, **`steps`**, **`confidence`**), we will now use that model to validate agent responses before our application consumes them. Pydantic's **`parse_raw`** and **`parse_obj`** methods make it easy to take raw model output (such as a JSON string) and enforce the schema rules we declared. If something is wrong, like missing fields, wrong types, incorrect structure, then the

Pydantic immediately raises a clear error that points exactly to the failure, which enables quick correction.

The given below is an example of validating the agent output from a model before we use it:

```
from pydantic import ValidationError
from src.output_schema import AgentOutput
def validate_agent_output(raw_text: str) -> AgentOutput:
    """
    Validates the raw JSON output returned by the agent model.
    Raises a clear error if validation fails.
    """
    try:
        validated = AgentOutput.parse_raw(raw_text)
        return validated
    except ValidationError as exc:
        # Here we raise or handle the validation error
explicitly
        print("ValidationError: Agent output did not match the
expected schema.")
        print(exc)
        raise
```

Now here, in the above validation code,

- We assume **`raw_text`** is a string response from the model that should contain valid JSON matching our schema.
- We call **`AgentOutput.parse_raw`**, which attempts to parse and validate the text according to our defined fields (**`answer`**, **`steps`**, **`confidence`**).
- If the input does not conform to the schema, Pydantic raises a **`ValidationError`** that includes detailed diagnostics about which fields were missing or which types were incorrect. And,
- We catch that exception and report it clearly before re-raising it or handling it in a higher-level logic (for example, prompting the model to retry with stricter instructions).

Imagine our agent returns the following raw JSON:

```
{
 "answer": "The total is 42",
 "steps": "We calculated it",
 "confidence": "high"
}
```

In it, we can see two failures:

1. **steps** should be a list of strings, not a single string.
2. **confidence** should be a float, not a string.

When we run this JSON through our validation function:

```
validate_agent_output(raw_json_string)
```

The Pydantic immediately raises a **ValidationError**, and the printed message will indicate exactly which type mismatches occurred and where. This clear, early failure saves time because we know exactly what is wrong and can fix the prompt or adjust the model instructions accordingly.

Handling Validation Errors in Agent Loop

In an interactive agent loop, we can integrate this validation routine so that the agent never proceeds with an invalid structure. See the following command:

```
try:
   validated_output = validate_agent_output(model_response)
except ValidationError:
   print("Agent returned invalid JSON. Please check the prompt
instructions or schema.")
   continue  # skip this response and allow for a retry
```

After running the above, we do not pass malformed data into our business logic. We also immediately notify users or developers that something went wrong. And, we do not attempt to unpack fields from a bad structure, which would cause deeper errors.

The Fail-fast behavior in this context means ***detect and stop at the first sign of structural error*** instead of allowing the program to run in an inconsistent state.

"Golden Prompt" Regression Test

In software development, ***regression testing*** is actually a practice of re-running trusted test cases after changes to ensure that previously working functionality has not been broken. It acts like a safety net that quickly flags unintended side effects when code evolves or underlying libraries change. In the context of AI agents, maintaining a set of fixed prompts with known, correct outputs lets us verify that the core behavior remains stable over time.

So here, a ***golden prompt regression test*** is one such simple test case where we define a fixed prompt that represents a critical use case, then validate that the agent's output continues to match our structured schema exactly. Such tests act as a quick check before and after changes, giving developers immediate feedback about unintended deviations.

Designing Regression Test

To keep things straightforward, our regression test will:

1. Define a fixed input prompt that represents a stable and important scenario.
2. Call the agent with that prompt, capturing the raw JSON output.

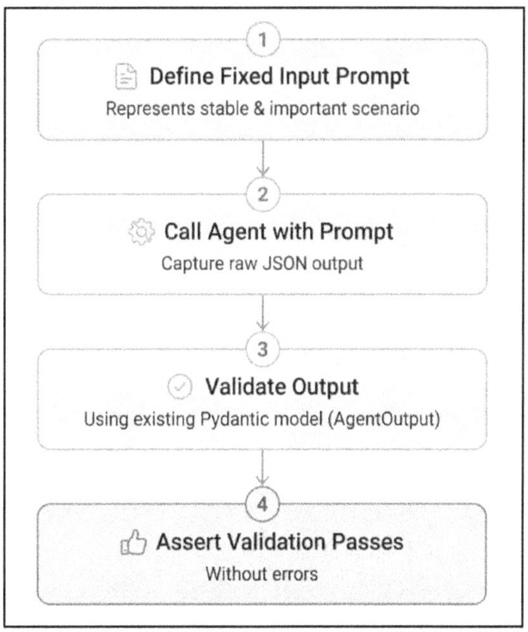

Fig 3.1 Regression Test Process for AI Agent

3. Validate the output using our existing Pydantic model (**`AgentOutput`**). And finally,
4. Assert that the validation passes without errors.

Writing Golden Prompt Test

As regular practice, we will create a new file **`tests/test_golden_prompt.py`** and will add the following regression test with the help of **unittest** framework and previously built **AgentOutput** Pydantic model.:

```
# tests/test_golden_prompt.py
import unittest
from src.output_schema import AgentOutput
from src.agent_client import run_agent_once
class TestGoldenPrompt(unittest.TestCase):
   def test_golden_prompt_schema(self):
       """
       This test sends a fixed prompt to the agent and ensures
       the output adheres to the AgentOutput schema.
       """
       # Define our golden prompt
       prompt = (
           "summarize: The team completed the project review.
"
           "We discussed next quarter goals and agreed on the
timeline."
       )
       # Run the agent once with that prompt
       raw_response = run_agent_once(prompt)
       # Validate using Pydantic model
       validated = AgentOutput.parse_raw(raw_response)
       # Assertions confirm schema fields are correct
       self.assertIsInstance(validated.answer, str)
       self.assertIsInstance(validated.steps, list)
       self.assertIsInstance(validated.confidence, float)
if __name__ == "__main__":
   unittest.main()
```

This above test does the following:

- It defines a ***golden prompt*** that represents a real scenario we care about.
- It calls a helper function **`run_agent_once`** (to be implemented in the code) that runs the agent with the prompt and returns the raw JSON string.
- It parses and validates the output using the **`AgentOutput`** Pydantic model. If any field is missing or has the wrong type, **`parse_raw`** will raise a validation error and the test will fail.

After this, we will simply run it:

```
python -m unittest tests/test_golden_prompt.py
```

If the result is successful, it means the agent's structured output still matches the expected schema for the golden prompt. When it fails, it means something has changed, either in the model or in the instructions around it. It gives us immediate feedback so we can check it out and fix it.

This simple test becomes part of our ***feedback loop*** as it runs quickly, validates contract compliance, and supports rapid iterations on models and prompts with confidence.

Summary

Quickly summarizing our key leaernings, starting with the limitations of natural language outputs for programmatic consumption and saw how defining a clear contract for data structure reduces ambiguity, making integration with code simple and robust. We discussed how JSON schemas, when paired with validation, create predictable and machine-friendly output that downstream logic can depend on without brittle ad-hoc parsing or fragile assumptions. The structured outputs helped prepare our application logic to work reliably across iterations of model changes without unexpected failures.

Later, we walked through how to define a Pydantic model to represent our agent's expected output, covering fields such as **`answer`**, **`steps`**, and **`confidence`**, and we practiced validating model responses against this schema in Python. This included enforcing valid JSON from the model with clear prompting and schema enforcement. We also learned how to integrate fast failure validation and handle errors when schema expectations were not met, ensuring that malformed data did not propagate further into business logic. Finally, we built a golden prompt regression test that runs a fixed prompt and asserts that the agent's output adheres to our structured schema.

Chapter 4: Switching Models without Rewriting Agent

Overview

In this chapter, we will learn to design our AI agent to support ***model switching without rewriting its logic***. We will explore the concept of a ***model gateway*** to isolate provider-specific details so that the rest of our agent logic remains untouched when we change models. We will walk through building a simple gateway, and then to route requests to different providers using configuration values, and lastly to normalize their outputs for structured validation.

Next, we will build a ***compare models*** runner that sends a single prompt to multiple configured models, saves their structured responses into separate JSON files, and facilitates side-by-side comparison. Finally, we will derive a ***compatibility checklist*** for evaluating new models quickly and systematically. This checklist will focus on key criteria like structured JSON stability, tool calling reliability, and latency, and show how to qualify new models in minutes using our existing tests. By the end of this chapter, we will be able to change and evaluate models confidently based on data rather than guesswork.

Exploring Model Gateway

In modern AI applications, especially those that use multiple large language models, direct integration with each provider's API quickly becomes a maintenance burden. Each vendor defines its own endpoints, authentication, request formats, and response structures. For example, OpenAI's API looks different from Anthropic's, and open-source engines or self-hosted services introduce their own nuances. So here, an elegant solution to this chaos is to introduce a ***model gateway***, a dedicated module that acts like a ***switchboard or traffic controller*** between our agent and the model providers.

A model gateway functions similarly to an API gateway in traditional software architectures, but for AI model interactions. It sits between the agent and multiple backend LLM services and exposes a single, consistent interface for model calls. The gateway handles all nuances such as authentication, payload transformation, provider-specific quirks, and routing decisions. This single point of contact lets us ***switch models or providers by changing configuration in the gateway*** rather than rewriting any agent code. With this, if we want to experiment with a new open-source model, move calls to a cheaper endpoint, or fall back to a different provider during outages, the gateway becomes the place for that logic. It ensures the core agent loop and business logic are staying stable.

Implement Model Gateway

A ***model gateway*** is a dedicated Python module that acts as the single interface between our agent loop and any number of underlying language model providers. Without a gateway, direct calls to different provider SDKs (e.g., OpenAI, Anthropic, local inference servers like vLLM) would scatter provider-specific details throughout our agent code. A model gateway hides those details behind a unified interface so that our agent code simply asks "run this prompt" and gets a structured result back, without knowing where the model lives or how it is invoked internally.

In our project, the ***model gateway module*** reads the configuration (like model name and API endpoint from our **`config.py`**), determines which model provider to call, formats the request appropriately, sends it, and then normalizes the response before handing it back to the agent loop. Hence, it is the ***single place*** for us to update wiring details such as provider SDKs or switching between cloud models and local models like vLLM. Rest all the other parts of the agent will remain untouched when such changes occur.

Preliminary Setup

We will put the gateway logic in **`model_gateway.py`** inside **`src`** folder:

Before writing any function in the file, we will import our existing **`config.py`** so that the gateway reads configuration such as **`MODEL_NAME`**, **`API_BASE_URL`**, and **`API_KEY`**. Since, the gateway talks to multiple providers, the model name format can include a provider namespace, e.g., **`"openai:gpt-4o"`** for OpenAI or **`"local:vllm-default"`** for a local server.

Implementing Gateway Interface

We will start with the basic imports:

```
# src/model_gateway.py
from typing import Dict
```

```
import json
from src.config import MODEL_NAME, API_BASE_URL, API_KEY
# We will import HTTP client libraries when needed, e.g.
requests or httpx
import requests
```

Now here, the gateway needs a function that accepts a prompt and returns the raw JSON response that the agent loop will later validate. So here, we will call **call_model**:

```
def call_model(prompt: str) -> str:
    """
    Calls the configured model with the given prompt
    and returns the raw JSON text response.
    """
    # Construct provider and model from a composite string like
"openai:gpt-4o"
    if ":" in MODEL_NAME:
        provider, model_name = MODEL_NAME.split(":", 1)
    else:
        provider, model_name = "openai", MODEL_NAME
    provider = provider.lower().strip()
    # Route to the appropriate provider implementation
    if provider == "openai":
        return _call_openai_model(model_name, prompt)
    elif provider == "local":
        return _call_local_model(model_name, prompt)
    else:
        raise RuntimeError(f"Unsupported provider: {provider}")
```

In the above, the **call_model** inspects **MODEL_NAME** to decide which path to invoke. That makes the gateway module aware of which provider is active.

Implementing OpenAI Model Calls

For cloud models that follow an OpenAI-like API, we can implement **_call_openai_model** using simple HTTP requests. We just have to send the prompt text to **API_BASE_URL** with proper authentication:

```
def _call_openai_model(model_name: str, prompt: str) -> str:
    url = f"{API_BASE_URL}/completions"
    headers = {
        "Authorization": f"Bearer {API_KEY}",
        "Content-Type": "application/json",
    }
    payload: Dict = {
        "model": model_name,
        "prompt": prompt,
        "max_tokens": 500,
        "temperature": 0.7,
    }
    response = requests.post(url, headers=headers,
json=payload)
    response.raise_for_status()
    return response.text
```

This above code posts the JSON with basic parameters to the model endpoint and returns the raw response text. And, this above interface can handle any provider that follows the OpenAI API structure if we point **API_BASE_URL** and set relevant keys.

Implementing vLLM Call

For a local inference engine such as vLLM, here we need to adjust the API call format to match the local server's protocol. It looks like a similar HTTP request if the server exposes a REST endpoint but for now, I will provide you with a placeholder function:

```
def _call_local_model(model_name: str, prompt: str) -> str:
    """
    Call a locally hosted model endpoint such as vLLM.
```

```
    The endpoint and calling format may vary depending on
setup.
    For now, treat it like an HTTP JSON interface.
    """
    url = f"{API_BASE_URL}/v1/completions"
    headers = {"Content-Type": "application/json"}
    payload: Dict = {
        "model": model_name,
        "prompt": prompt,
    }
    response = requests.post(url, headers=headers,
json=payload)
    response.raise_for_status()
    return response.text
```

This above function may change depending on the local model's or vLLMs API.

Updating Agent Loop for Gateway Use

Since, the gateway is exposing the **call_model**, we can now update the **agent_loop.py** so that when the decision logic chooses a model inference path, it calls the gateway rather than hard-coding a provider SDK as shown below:

```
from src.model_gateway import call_model
# inside run_agent loop
tool_request, final_text = decide(user_prompt)
if tool_request is None:
    raw_response = call_model(user_prompt)
    # validate and parse with Pydantic here...
```

This line is minimal because all provider differences are encapsulated in the gateway. If tomorrow we switch from an OpenAI model to a local vLLM server, the only change we need to make is in **config.py**, where we need to update the **MODEL_NAME** and **API_BASE_URL**. You do not have to do anything else, even in the agent loop. This is another reason why we call it as ***unified switchboard interface***.

If there are any enhancements like retries, fallback strategies, observability, and batching are required, then they can be added inside the gateway itself without touching the agent logic.

Swapping Models

In this topic, we will learn to ***run same agent using different models*** simply by changing configuration values, without altering the core agent logic. To do this, when we change **`MODEL_NAME`** and **`API_BASE_URL`** in our config, the agent begins using a different backend model provider or endpoint. This allows us to try with new models or switch between hosted cloud models and local model servers without rewriting any part of our agent logic. It also prepares the agent codebase for future model upgrades and fallbacks with minimal effort.

Changing Configuration

If we just revisit in the past chapter, regarding the **`model_gateway.py`**, we parse the model identifier from the configuration values defined in **`config.py`**. And then, the gateway reads a composite string like **`openai:gpt-4o`** or **`local:meta-llama-7b`** from **`MODEL_NAME`** and routes the call to the appropriate handler. This means that the same function call **`call_model(prompt)`** can execute against different backends based purely on the name and endpoint values in config. And this flexibility is a major advantage.

So, instead of rewriting API calls, request payloads, and credential handling every time we change models, we just have to ***update environment variables***, and the gateway adapts at runtime.

Running Agent with Two Different Models

We will explore it now through a quick example. In the following, we will set up our environment and config for one model, and will take cloud provider as a choice.

As a first stpe, we will export the environment variables and run the script:

```
export MODEL_NAME="openai:gpt-5.2"
export API_BASE_URL="https://api.openai.com/v1"
export OPENAI_API_KEY="YOUR_OPENAI_KEY"
python scripts/run_agent.py
```

Once we do it, the agent starts using the model named **`gpt-5.2`** via the OpenAI API gateway. When the agent calls **`call_model`**, the gateway reads the provider prefix and routes the request appropriately without the agent loop being aware of the details.

Now, consider that we want to switch from a cloud provider to a ***local inference server***, I mean the vLLM:

So, for this, I will now export new environment variables:

```
export MODEL_NAME="local:meta-llama-13b-instruct"
export API_BASE_URL="http://localhost:8000/v1"
python scripts/run_agent.py
```

Now here, because vLLM exposes an OpenAI-compatible server interface, the same gateway logic interacts with it by simply changing the **API_BASE_URL** to point to the local endpoint and setting the **MODEL_NAME** to a local model identifier. This teaches us to carry out the ***model switching with just a config***, while we keep the agent loop and gateway code unchanged.

In addition, even if we want to test cost, latency, or performance differences between such models, this can be easily done with just a simple update **MODEL_NAME** and then running the same agent. There are no code rewrites at all. Such a flexibility and conveneience reduces bugs, accelerates development, and supports continuous integration practices.

Model Comparison Tool

We will now move on to building a ***model comparison runner.*** Its purpose is to send the same prompt to multiple models and captures their structured responses as JSON. And then we can compare models side-by-side to decide which model performs better across output quality, stability, and schema adherence. If we make such task repeatable, then it is will help us to establish output baselines, detect regressions, and reason about trade-offs between cost, latency, and quality when switching between model providers or versions.

To start with, I will brief you how this model compsarison tool functions:

Capability of Compare Runner

A compare runner is a standalone script or function that:

- Accepts a single ***fixed prompt*** representing the task or use case to evaluate.
- Iterates over a list of ***model configurations***.
- Sends the prompt to each model via the ***model gateway*** which we built earlier.
- Parses and validates the model's JSON output against our Pydantic schema.
- Saves the ***raw*** and ***validated*** outputs to JSON files for inspection. And finally,
- Summarizes the differences across outputs so we can inspect them manually or programmatically.

Once we run it, it gives us a ***baseline comparison dataset*** which we can extend with automatic scoring later.

Compare Runner Script

We will create a file **compare_models.py** and it will have the following script:

```
# compare_models.py
import os
import json
from datetime import datetime
from src.model_gateway import call_model
from src.output_schema import AgentOutput, ValidationError
# List of model names we want to compare
MODELS_TO_COMPARE = [
    "openai:gpt-5.2",
    "openai:gpt-4o-mini",
    "local:meta-llama-13b-instruct",
]
# Fixed prompt for comparison
PROMPT = (
    "summarize: The team completed the project review. "
    "We discussed next quarter goals and agreed on the
timeline."
)
# Directory to store results
OUTPUT_DIR = "model_comparison_outputs"
os.makedirs(OUTPUT_DIR, exist_ok=True)
def run_comparison():
    report = {}
    timestamp = datetime.utcnow().strftime("%Y%m%dT%H%M%SZ")
    for model_name in MODELS_TO_COMPARE:
        print(f"Running comparison for model: {model_name}")
        # Set config values dynamically
```

```
        os.environ["MODEL_NAME"] = model_name
        # Get raw response via gateway
        raw_response = call_model(PROMPT)
        # Try to validate it against the schema
        try:
            validated = AgentOutput.parse_raw(raw_response)
            status = "valid"
            parsed = validated.dict()
        except ValidationError as exc:
            status = "invalid"
            parsed = {"error": str(exc)}
        # Store results
        filename =
f"{model_name.replace(':','_')}_{timestamp}.json"
        filepath = os.path.join(OUTPUT_DIR, filename)
        record = {
            "model": model_name,
            "raw_response": raw_response,
            "status": status,
            "parsed_output": parsed,
        }
        with open(filepath, "w") as f:
            json.dump(record, f, indent=2)
        report[model_name] = filepath
        print(f"Saved results for {model_name} -> {filepath}")
    # Print summary of saved files
    print("\nComparison completed. Outputs saved:")
    for k, v in report.items():
        print(f"{k}: {v}")
```

```
if __name__ == "__main__":
    run_comparison()
```

The above script is quite long so I will quickly brief you what it is:

- The ***MODELS_TO_COMPARE*** is a list of model identifiers which we are aiming to evaluate.
- The ***PROMPT*** is the fixed string we will send to every model.
- Each model is invoked by setting the **`MODEL_NAME`** environment variable before calling **`call_model`**.
- We validate the response using **`AgentOutput.parse_raw`**. If the output fails schema validation, we mark it as **`"invalid"`**, which helps with comparing schema stability.
- Finally, the results are saved in a JSON file under **`model_comparison_outputs`**.

After running the script, we will see files like:

```
model_comparison_outputs/openai_gpt-5.2_20260304T120000Z.json
model_comparison_outputs/openai_gpt-4o-mini_20260304T120000Z.json
model_comparison_outputs/local_meta-llama-13b-instruct_20260304T120000Z.json
```

Each of the above file will contain ***raw_response*** that tells unvalidated model output text, ***status*** of whether the output matched the expected schema, and the ***parsed_output*** basically the validated JSON object or the schema errors.

This side-by-side format is the basis for deeper comparisons and accordingly, we can select the models that are reliable for the said use case.

Model Evaluation and Scoring Checklist

A new model might have great raw language skills, but if it doesn't consistently call tools, deviates from the required JSON schemas, or has unacceptable latency, it'll degrade the reliability of the agent application. Hence, whenever any new model is added to an agent system, it's important to make sure that it works well with the architecture we have got in place. There is something called ***compatibility checklist*** to help us figure out if a model is a good fit for our agent's needs. This checklist focuses on what matters for our specific needs, like reliable tool calling, consistent JSON output, or acceptable latency.

Model Compatibility Checklist

I have drafted a checklist to the best of my understanding. You can use it to evaluate any new model before we adopt it in the agent:

1. Structured Output Reliability

- Does the model ***consistently*** return valid JSON matching our schema (e.g., **`answer`**, **`steps`**, **`confidence`**)?
- Does the output require minimal or no post-processing before schema validation?
- Does the model respect our strict prompt instructions for structured JSON?
- If the model frequently deviates (extra text, malformed JSON), it signals poor fit.

2. Tool Calling Accuracy

- Is the model reliably triggering correct tools based on intent (e.g., **`summarize_text`** or **`calc`** tools)?
- For a set of known tool-call prompts, does the model correctly format tool arguments?
- Does the model avoid hallucinatory tool requests (curated test prompts from our regression suite help catch this)?
- Tool reliability often predicts real-world stability of agent workflows.

3. Latency and Performance

- Is the model fast enough for our expected use case?
- Do average and worst-case response times stay within acceptable limits for responsiveness?
- Are token costs and compute usage reasonable relative to our usage profile?
- Latency impacts user experience and real-time workflows, so this must be measured.

4. Schema Adherence Rate

- What percentage of responses pass our structured schema validation in our regression tests?
- Are there patterns where the model repeatedly fails specific fields or types?
- A high schema pass rate indicates a model that integrates smoothly with our validation logic.

5. Stability Across Runs

- Does the model produce consistent structure and similar content for repeated identical prompts?

- Does output variability stay within acceptable limits (e.g., confidence scores and steps structure)?
- Stability ensures predictable behavior in automated workflows, reducing debugging friction.

6. Tool Integration Robustness

- Does the model correctly sequence tool calls in multi-step prompts?
- Can it maintain tool call coherence across agent iterations?
- Complex agent workflows often require multi-turn reasoning. A model that fails sequencing during tests likely causes errors in production.

If we could recall the ***golden prompt regression tests,*** we can use it along with the ***model comparison runner***, and then we can use it with the checklist quickly. This whole approach lets us choose models that perform well in isolation and integrate robustly into the agent workflows.

Summary

To sum up, we learned to design the agent with model switching capability without touching the core logic. We explored ***model gateway*** and learned to keep the agent loop model-agnostic. We then learned to implement the gateway, integrate it into our agent loop, and then to validate its behavior by swapping models using environment variables only.

Later, we created a ***model comparison runner*** that executed the same prompt across multiple models and stored structured results as JSON files so that side-by-side comparison became easy. We also derived a ***compatibility checklist*** for evaluating new models quickly, focusing on structured output reliability, tool calling accuracy, schema validation rates, latency, and stability. This chapter equipped us with patterns and practical scripts that helped standardize model switching, evaluation, and qualification.

CHAPTER 5: RUNNING vLLM

Overview

In this chapter, we will focus on running our agent ***locally*** using ***vLLM***. We will learn the working of vLLM as a local inference backend with whom the existing model gateway and agent loop can talk, without any code changes. We will explore vLLM in one sentence too.

Later, we will get hands-on, wherein, we will start the vLLM using **`vllm serve`**, and then to confirm the server is responding correctly to requests from any HTTP client. You will update the configuration so that the model gateway points at **`http://localhost:8000/v1`**, and we will rerun the agent script to ***confirm structured outputs and tool integrations working exactly as we intend to***. And lastly, we will explore performance measurements, such as capturing wall-clock latency, to help us compare response times between hosted and local backends without needing a complex observability stack.

Exploring vLLM Integration

The vLLMs are a high-performance, local inference server that exposes an OpenAI-compatible API. It allows us to run large language models on our own machine in the exact same way the code talks to cloud providers. Here, we actually get the ***interface standardization*** we rely on in our model gateway, endpoints like **`/v1/chat/completions`** and **`/v1/completions`**, but backed by a ***locally hosted model instance*** instead of a hosted cloud LLM. This allows us to ***swap between the hosted and local models by configuration alone*** without rewriting any agent logic.

So, in this, when we install and launch vLLM's OpenAI-compatible server locally with **`vllm serve <model-name>`**, it spins up an HTTP interface that mimics the standard API the agent expects. And then, we can point the same gateway and agent config at **`http://localhost:8000/v1`** instead of a cloud URL, and the agent will work the same way, only now that the inference runs on our own hardware. This means any environment where the agent runs can choose between cloud hosting, private servers, or on-device inference simply by adjusting **API_BASE_URL** and **MODEL_NAME**.

In the following, I am providing you a simple diagram showing how vLLM fits into our agent architecture:

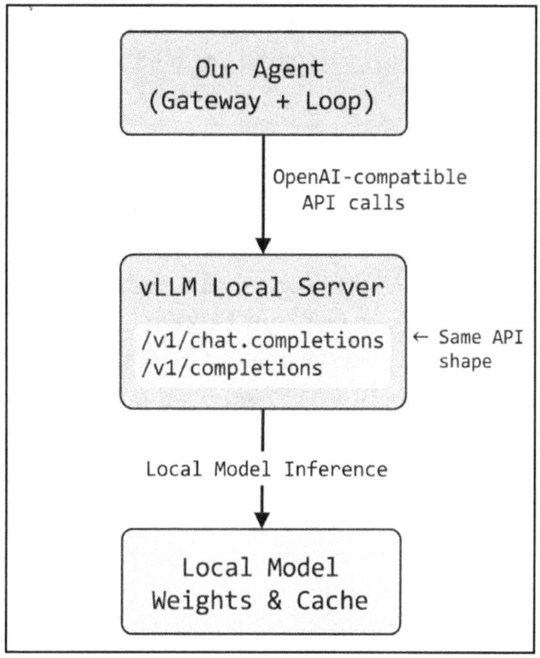

Fig 5.1 vLLM Integration Architecture

What matters here is that ***vLLM's API speaks the same language the agent expects***. This is the real key to run the agent code ***unchanged*** whether the backend is a hosted OpenAI model or a local one hosted with vLLM. We just need to change the configuration and endpoint. You get all the benefits of local control, faster inference for some workloads, data privacy, reduced cost, without changing any of the agent's code.

Initializing vLLM

Here, we will ***practically*** run the server on our machine, point the **model gateway** to that local endpoint, and confirm that it is responding to requests. Since, the vLLM implements standard OpenAI API endpoints such as **`/v1/completions`** and **`/v1/chat/completions`**, our existing agent code and gateway works unchanged, only the base URL shifts from cloud to **`localhost`**. That is the essence of running locally with minimal changes.

So here, we will start the vLLM server, test the endpoint manually with a simple request, then update our config so the gateway points to the local base URL. It gives us immediate feedback that the local server is reachable, and confirms that our agent does not need code rewrites to switch between hosted and local model backends.

Running vLLM Server Locally

To run vLLM as a local API server that speaks the OpenAI-compatible interface, we use the

vllm serve command with the chosen model's name. This command loads the model and starts an API server listening on a port (by default port 8000).

Given below is the starting command:

```
vllm serve meta-llama/Llama-3.1-8B-Instruct
```

This is the basic invocation that tells vLLM to serve the **meta-llama/Llama-3.1-8B-Instruct** model over an HTTP API at **http://localhost:8000/v1**. You might need to provide additional flags such as **--api-key token123** if the client expects an API key, or **--host 0.0.0.0** to expose the server beyond localhost. The important point is that this command boots up an OpenAI-compatible API server that supports both chat and completion endpoints out of the box.

Once the server starts, it will print logs indicating model loading status and the port it is listening on. By default, the OpenAI-compatible API surface will appear at **http://localhost:8000/v1**, so we can call standard OpenAI endpoints against it.

Quick Smoke Test

Before wiring this local server into our agent, we want to confirm that the server accepts requests and responds. And, the simplest way to check is using a HTTP client like **curl** from a separate terminal as shown below:

```
curl http://localhost:8000/v1/chat/completions \
 -H "Content-Type: application/json" \
 -d '{
       "model":"meta-llama/Llama-3.1-8B-Instruct",
       "messages":[{"role":"user","content":"Hello from local
vLLM!"}],
       "max_tokens":50
     }'
```

In the above, if everything is correct, we should see a JSON response with text generated by the model. Because the vLLM implements the OpenAI API protocol, the response shape should look like what we would get from a cloud provider, which makes the output easy to validate in the same way we validate remote models.

If the server does not respond or returns errors, we then need to check that the vLLM process is still running and that the model loaded successfully.

Pointing Model Gateway to Local Endpoint

We will now update the agent's configuration so that **`API_BASE_URL`** points at the vLLM server instead of a cloud provider. For this, we will set as below:

```
export API_BASE_URL="http://localhost:8000/v1"
export MODEL_NAME="local:meta-llama/Llama-3.1-8B-Instruct"
```

In the above, the **`MODEL_NAME`** prefix **`local:`** is just a convention used in our model gateway logic to differentiate local from other providers. Once these values are in place, our ***model gateway*** will route calls to the local vLLM server and treat them as though they were remote OpenAI API calls, because vLLM's API surface is standard. This switch is entirely configuration-driven, the agent loop and gateway code do not change at all.

After exporting the environment variables, we then must run the agent as normal:

```
python scripts/run_agent.py
```

After this, the agent should send requests to the local vLLM server through **`call_model`**, and we will see the model responses come back through the gateway exactly as before. What makes this possible is the ***OpenAI API compatibility*** that vLLM exposes.

In later topics we will use this pattern to explore latency comparisons, offline development setups, and cost-effective local inference patterns, all while keeping our agent logic stable.

Agent Switching and Portability

We will now move on to explore the switching of our agent from a hosted cloud model to this local setup, which just requires ***only one configuration change***. Since, the vLLM exposes an API that matches the standard OpenAI completions and chat endpoints, our existing agent and ***model gateway*** continue to work the same, without modifying any logic in the agent loop or gateway code.

So here in this topic, we will learn to experiment with changing the ***base URL*** to point at local vLLM server, and then we will re-run the agent script, and ***confirm the tools and structured JSON validation continue to work effortlessly***.

Updating Config for Local vLLM

The only changes we make are to the ***environment configuration*** that our gateway reads at runtime. Previously when using a hosted cloud model, the environment looked like this:

```
export API_BASE_URL="https://api.openai.com/v1"
```

```
export MODEL_NAME="openai:gpt-5.2"
export OPENAI_API_KEY="YOUR_OPENAI_KEY"
```

Now, to point the agent at a ***local vLLM server***, we need to update base URL and model name:

```
export API_BASE_URL="http://localhost:8000/v1"
export MODEL_NAME="local:meta-llama/Llama-3.1-8B-Instruct"
# Set API key to a non-empty string if vLLM requires one
export API_KEY="my-local-key"
```

After this, the **API_BASE_URL** now references the local vLLM server's OpenAI-compatible port. The **MODEL_NAME** prefix **local:** is simply how our gateway differentiates local routing, but the rest of our agent logic still calls **call_model(prompt)** with the same interface.

Re-Running Agent without Code Changes

Once the environment is set, we can then re-run the agent:

```
python scripts/run_agent.py
```

Now, since we pointed model gateway's to **http://localhost:8000/v1**, every call that the gateway makes goes to the local vLLM server. The gateway constructs requests just as it did before based on **MODEL_NAME** and prompt input and sends them to the local endpoint. The agent loop receives output text back from vLLM, and because the responses follow the same OpenAI-compatible JSON shapes, the ***structured JSON parsing and Pydantic validation*** continue to work without any code adaptations.

So here, for example, if the agent makes a call such as:

```
raw_response = call_model("summarize: Explain structured
outputs")
```

The, the response will come from **localhost:8000** and still resolves to valid JSON that fits the defined schema (**answer**, **steps**, **confidence**). And, the tools like summarizer and calculator still integrate visibly downstream because the structured output remains consistent.

This seamless swap demonstrates the key value of the design: ***no rewrites***. You retain the same agent behaviors and structured output validation whether using cloud models or self-hosted vLLM. The only line that changed was where the client directs its requests, a powerful technique when building portable, flexible, and provider-agnostic agent systems.

Measuring Agent Performance

When we run agent against different backends, whether hosted cloud model or the vLLM, if we get to know ***how fast*** the responses come back, it does helps to make practical decisions about which setup suits our need.

Now here, we do not need a full observability stack like the metrics dashboards, distributed tracing, and so on. We can just start with lightweight timing measurements such as ***wall-clock time*** captured directly in Python. The wall-clock time basically reflects the elapsed time from "send" to "receive," including network overhead and model inference latency, and can be measured simply using functions like **`time.time()`** or more precise alternatives like **`time.perf_counter()`** from Python's standard library.

So, in the following, we will do the wall-clock measurements, model benchmarking, and then we will see how the results look like.

Measuring Wall-Clock Time

So here, we will use the built-in **`time`** module or **`perf_counter`** to get the high-resolution timing:

```
import time
start_time = time.perf_counter()
raw_response = call_model(prompt)  # send to gateway
end_time = time.perf_counter()
elapsed = end_time - start_time
print(f"Elapsed time: {elapsed:.3f} seconds")
```

In the above script, the **`time.perf_counter()`** gives us a high-resolution timestamp before and after the request, and the difference is the ***wall-clock time*** for the entire call. This includes network latency, server processing, and the client's overhead. Because it is a simple subtraction of two timestamps, it is appropriate for rough comparisons without specialized instrumentation.

If we want even more precision for repeated small invocations, we can use the **`timeit`** module, but for network-bound calls such as API requests to vLLM or hosted models, the simple start/stop pattern above is both easier and sufficiently informative.

Benchmarking across Models

Using the same timing code, we can extend the ***compare models runner*** from the previous chapter to measure latencies systematically. We can record the elapsed time for each model invocation and add it to the comparison output file, as shown below:

```
import time
# inside comparison loop
start_time = time.time()
raw_response = call_model(PROMPT)
elapsed_time = time.time() - start_time
record["latency"] = elapsed_time
```

As shown above, each model's performance is captured alongside its structured output. And, we can have a simple JSON entry like the following:

```
{
 "model": "local:meta-llama-13b-instruct",
 "status": "valid",
 "latency": 0.87,
 "parsed_output": { ... }
}
```

When we run the same prompt multiple times against both a hosted cloud model and the local vLLM setup, we will be able to ***compare relative latency*** across different backends. This gives us actionable information, such as whether running locally reduces network overhead or if a hosted service responds faster under certain conditions.

With these simple metrics in place, we can start comparing not just correctness and structure, but also how responsive the agent feels under different configurations, an important step toward production-ready agent applications.

Summary

To conclude, we learned to run agent locally using ***vLLM***, and we could switch backends without rewriting any agent logic. We learned about vLLM as a local HTTP server that speaks the same API surface our model gateway and agent loop expect. We then ***practically ran*** the vLLM server locally on **`http://localhost:8000/v1`**, confirmed that it responded to standard requests, and updated our **`API_BASE_URL`** and **`MODEL_NAME`** config to point at this local server instead of a hosted cloud model.

Next, we demonstrated ***switching our agent from hosted cloud to local inference by changing only the base URL and model name in config***. We then covered simple ***performance measurement techniques*** like capturing wall-clock time to compare latency across backends without a full observability stack. The whole chapter reinforced that a design strategy based on API compatibility and centralized model gateway hlpes us with a portable and flexible agent deployments that adapt from cloud to local environments with minimal-to-zero friction.

CHAPTER 6: DESIGNING STABLE BUSINESS LOGIC ACROSS MULTIPLE SDKS

Overview

In this chapter, we will focus on designing the agent. We will leanr to keep the ***core business logic stable*** across different SDKs. So here, we are going to learn to isolate SDK wiring behind ***runtime adapters*** so that the core, including tools, structured output schemas, and prompt definitions, remains untouched and agnostic of execution engines. We will explore ***Adapter Pattern*** and learn to glue incompatible interfaces without the underlying logic. We will model the SDKs to swap, upgrade, or experiment with different providers without rewriting the core agent.

Next, we will build an ***Agent App Core*** module encapsulating all the stable elements of our agent, structured schemas, tool contracts, prompt templates, and high-level orchestration logic, and keep it independent from any SDK specifics. We will connect the core with ***OpenAI Agents SDK*** using an adapter layer. Later, we then build a ***second runtime adapter*** for an alternative SDK and reuse the same core logic with it. Overall, we will be learning to architect the agent so well, such that the business logic survives SDK churn and able to support long-term maintainability.

SDKs as Runtimes

In the world of AI and agent development, the SDKs for model providers and agent frameworks are set to evolve rapidly. And, the newer versions are getting shipped very frequently as providers add features, refine APIs, and introduce new capabilities in a very small period. This pace of change, often called ***SDK churn***. And it creates maintenance headaches if the core business logic is tightly coupled to a particular SDK's API, method signatures, or request/response shapes. For example, some agent frameworks and SDKs have suffered breaking changes and weak governance as they iterate for new features, which means modules that interact directly with them may require rewrites when those SDKs update.

However, such SDK churn is not unique to AI. In mature software engineering disciplines, frameworks and libraries change over time as well, but a well-designed system isolates such ***business logic*** from the ***infrastructure concerns*** such as SDK interfaces. There are various architectural patterns like layered or hexagonal, which are designed to enforce such separation. They encapsulate the external dependencies, including SDKs, APIs, and data sources, behind ***adapter layers***, and thereby the core business logic remains untouched when those dependencies evolve.

SDKs not part of Architecture

A key insight we want to carry forward is that SDKs should be treated as ***runtimes or execution engines*** rather than architectural pillars. An SDK provides concrete implementations for calling services, managing connections, and handling low-level details. But the ***core logic, the reasoning flow, tool contracts, structured output validation, and agent orchestration, should remain independent of the specific SDK used to perform those calls.*** When we embed SDK-specific APIs throughout the agent logic, the moment that SDK changes we are forced to change the business logic, a sign of poor separation of concerns.

Instead, we should design with an ***adapter or abstraction layer*** that sits between the core logic and the SDK. That layer is responsible for translating generic calls from the agent (for example, "call model with prompt X" or "execute tool Y") into SDK calls, handling provider details such as authentication, request formatting, streaming, and polling. The adapter acts like an "anti-corruption" layer, a term in software architecture that means isolating the rest of the system from external complexities, keeping SDK quirks out of the core modules.

SDK Isolation

And SDKs aren't part of our architecture. If you isolate SDK-specific wiring behind a dedicated adapter or gateway layer, the agent's business logic stays stable even when the underlying SDK changes. If a provider updates its library or changes the shape of an API call, we only need to update the adapter, not the entire agent loop and orchestration logic. That way, there's less chance of errors, it's easier to maintain, and we can support multiple SDKs (like OpenAI Agents SDK, Google ADK, and custom clients) through the same interface without having to use if/else checks all over the place.

From a software architecture perspective, it's similar to patterns like ***ports and adapters*** or ***clean architecture***, where the core domain (business logic) is separated from external systems like databases, web interfaces, or SDKs. When things change on the outside, it doesn't affect the inside because the dependencies flow out. It's not like the business logic depends on how those SDKs work on the inside. With such a mental model in use, our all the SDK interactions become concerns of the ***adapter/gateway layer***. And, the updating or swapping of SDKs becomes an isolated task that does not touch the agent's decision loop, tool integration logic, or structured output handling.

Building "Agent App Core" Module

We learned in the previous topic, that it is best to isolate the SDK-specific wiring behind well-defined boundaries. So, in our agent project, we will have the ***Agent App Core module*** to play that isolating role. It will try to centralize all the ***stable, business-centric pieces*** like tools, schemas, prompt definitions, and high-level model invocation logic, so that the surrounding infrastructure like the SDKs remains a pluggable "outer layer."

'Agent App Core' Components

The Agent App Core module functions as the ***trusted spine*** of the agent application. It contains:

- ***Tool Definitions and Contracts*** that includes calculator, summarizer, and other tools with strict input/output schemas.

- ***Structured Output Schemas*** like the Pydantic model that define what shapes agent responses and tool outputs must satisfy.
- ***Prompt Templates*** which include the reusable prompt texts that guide model behavior and structured output requirements.
- ***Gateway Interfaces*** that abstract provider and SDK differences behind one function call (e.g., `call_model`).
- ***Decision Logic*** which is the agent loop and reasoning flow that decides when to call tools or models based on user input.

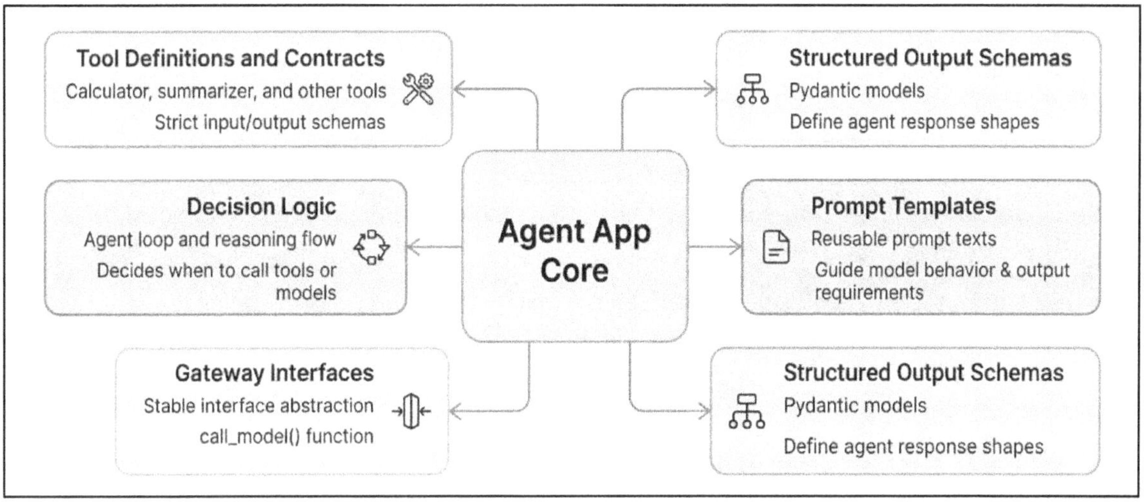

Fig 6.1 'Agent App Core' Key Components

After we encapsulate everything that is essential to the agent's functionality in one place, we can make logic ***independent from whichever SDK or client library we use*** to talk to model providers.

Structuring 'Agent App Core'

We will have a proper directory that encapsulates all ***business logic and agent rules***, separate from SDK clients. Following is my best advice to you:

```
src/
├── agent_core/
│   ├── __init__.py
│   ├── tools.py
│   ├── schemas.py
│   ├── prompts.py
│   └── orchestrator.py
├── model_gateway.py
├── config.py
└── tools/
```

The above structure isolates the ***business-level modules*** (**`agent_core`**) from SDK integrations (**`model_gateway`**) and external tools. The core module is where we define the capabilities and rules that never change even when SDKs do.

After this, within the **`tools.py`** and **`schemas.py`**, we will define only the core agent behavior and schemas without importing or depending on specific SDKs. For example, the Pydantic models and tool functions stay, and they are referenced by both the agent loop and the SDK adapter outside the core.

Also, the prompt templates should be written generically, without referencing any provider SDK. Their only dependency should be the interface the gateway exposes. It will thereby isolate the prompt logic from provider quirks and can keep the content stable. Over the period, this Agent App Core will sincerely serve us as durable, technology-agnostic, and insulated from change in external libraries.

Running Core with OpenAI Agents SDK

We will now ***practically connect our previously developed Agent App Core*** module to ***OpenAI Agents SDK***, and then we will run familiar tasks, like structured inference and tool invocation, using this SDK. Just to let you know, that the OpenAI Agents SDK provides primitives such as ***Agent*** and ***Runner*** to wrap model logic, instructions, and tools into a single executable object. And this allows us to leverage the SDK's features like automatic loop handling and structured tool calling without changing the ***architectural core*** of our agent logic.

Since, we deliberately isolated the business-centric code, tools, schemas, prompts, and gateway interfaces, in our ***Agent App Core***, we then must provide ***adapters or hooks*** to comply with the SDK's integration correctly. The core logic, orchestrator, prompt templates, structured JSON validation, does not need to change when we switch to using the Agents SDK as a runtime.

Installing OpenAI Agents SDK

We will install the Agents SDK very easily with the following command:

```
pip install openai-agents
```

It will provide us classes such as **`Agent`** and **`Runner`** along with tooling support for structured flows. Once installed, we can import the following constructs:

```
from agents import Agent, Runner
```

The SDK expects us to define an **`Agent`** with a name, instructions, model identifier, and an optional list of tools it can call. We can reference the core tools and structured output schemas here as the SDK will wire them into the agent run loop.

Wrapping Core into Agent

Next, we will write the following:

```
from agents import Agent, function_tool
from src.agent_core.prompts import DEFAULT_INSTRUCTIONS
from src.agent_core.tools import calc, summarize_text
# Wrap core tools as SDK tools
@function_tool
def calculator_tool(expression: str) -> str:
   return calc(expression)
@function_tool
def summarizer_tool(text: str) -> str:
   return summarize_text(text)
# Define the SDK agent
sdk_agent = Agent(
   name="CoreAgent",
   instructions=DEFAULT_INSTRUCTIONS,
   tools=[calculator_tool, summarizer_tool],
   model="gpt-5.2"  # or config-driven model name
```

```
)
```

From the above code, we are ***bridging*** the core tools into SDK tool decorators (**`@function_tool`**). By doing this, the agent SDK understands them. The **`instructions`** reference the prompt templates in our core module, maintaining stable behavior definitions. The SDK's **`Agent`** now knows how to use our core tools in its internal run orchestration.

Running Agent with SDK Runner

The Agents SDK uses **`Runner`** to execute an agent given some user input. We can prefer to choose to run synchronously as below:

```
result = Runner.run_sync(sdk_agent, "calculate: 2 + 2 then summarize the result")
print(result.final_output)
```

After running it, the SDK's runner will:

- Invoke the LLM for the initial prompt,
- Detect if a tool was called,
- Run the tool,
- Provide the tool output back to the model, and
- Continue until a final structured output is produced.

After doing this, our ***core logic, tools and structured output schemas, remains exactly the same***. We just handed them to the SDK as part of an **`Agent`** construct and allowed the SDK manage the execution flow.

This whole practice allows our core of the application to evolve, and independent of execution engine.

Creating Second Runtime Adapter

In the previous topic, we learned to plug the Core into one SDK's runtime ***without changing our core logic***. Now, we will learn to reuse that ***same core module*** with a ***different SDK runtime***. And, we will achieve it by writing a simple and a minimal ***runtime adapter*** to connect the core's stable interfaces to new SDK's expectations. And for your knowledge, this is exactly the purpose of the ***Adapter Pattern*** to make incompatible interfaces compatible without modifying the underlying core logic.

So, we will now create a lightweight adapter that acts as a ***bridge between the core's abstractions*** and the new SDK's runtime functions.

Purpose of Runtime Adapter

A ***runtime adapter*** adapts or wraps the API of a specific SDK to match the interface expected by the Agent App Core. In our project:

- The core expects a function like **`execute_model(prompt)`** that returns structured JSON results.
- The core expects tools as plain Python callables with known inputs and outputs. And,
- It expects a model invocation flow that ultimately produces JSON validated by Pydantic models.

A runtime adapter implements the ***SDK's unique API calls and protocols*** under the hood and maps them onto these expectations. The core does ***not*** import or depend on the SDK directly. It just calls the adapter, and nothing more.

Alternative SDK Adapter

For this, we will create **`other_sdk_adapter.py`** which sits outside the core but implements the interface the core relies on.

```
# src/other_sdk_adapter.py
from other_sdk import OtherAgentClient  # hypothetical SDK
client
from src.agent_core.prompts import DEFAULT_INSTRUCTIONS
from src.agent_core.tools import get_registered_tools
class OtherSDKAdapter:
   def __init__(self, model_name: str, api_key: str):
       self.client = OtherAgentClient(model=model_name,
api_key=api_key)
   def execute(self, prompt: str) -> str:
       """
       Execute the prompt via the alternative SDK and return
raw JSON text.
       """
       # The OtherAgentSDK might accept a workflow definition
or instructions
```

```
        # differently than the OpenAI Agents SDK. We adapt
here.
        response = self.client.run(
            instructions=DEFAULT_INSTRUCTIONS,
            prompt=prompt,
            tools=get_registered_tools(),
        )
        # Assume `response.json()` gives us structured JSON
text compatible
        # with our core's Pydantic schema
        return response.json()
```

Now, let me explain you what we are doing in this adapter:

- We import the alternative SDK in the adapter module, and isolating it from the core.
- We then reuse ***core prompt templates*** (**DEFAULT_INSTRUCTIONS**) and ***tool definitions*** (**get_registered_tools()**) from the **agent_core**.
- We expose method **execute(prompt)**. And,
- Internally, we call **OtherAgentClient** from other SDK, but that does ***not leak*** into the core logic.

So, even if the **OtherAgentSDK** changes its API tomorrow, we just need to update the **other_sdk_adapter.py**. We do not refactor the core at all.

Using Alternative Runtime Adapter

Next, the agent loop or the gateway can now function based on the configuration as shown below:

```
from src.other_sdk_adapter import OtherSDKAdapter
from src.config import MODEL_NAME, API_KEY
adapter = OtherSDKAdapter(model_name=MODEL_NAME,
api_key=API_KEY)
raw_output = adapter.execute("summarize: explain adapter
pattern simply")
validated = AgentOutput.parse_raw(raw_output)
print(validated)
```

This above code shows the resue of the stable **`AgentOutput`** schema from the core and the structured prompt templates. And, the actual ***runtime execution happens through the alternative SDK*** via the adapter. The core code does not know or care which SDK is executing. It just simply receives the structured JSON.

Overall, the only change to support an alternative SDK is to write an adapter that translates between the SDK's API and the stable interface, which the core expects.

Summary

Ito sum up our learnings, we learned to keep the ***business logic stable*** while supporting multiple SDKs as runtimes rather than baking provider-specific details into the core of our agent application. We explored why SDKs often change rapidly and how that creates ***churn*** if an application's logic is tightly coupled to a particular library or framework. To mitigate that, we treated SDKs as ***runtimes***, interchangeable execution engines, and built an architectural layer that isolates SDK specifics away from the core agent logic. This isolation was achieved by centralizing stable components such as tools, structured schemas, prompt templates, and orchestrator logic into an ***Agent App Core*** module, with SDK-dependent wiring confined to dedicated adapter layers. This strategy ensured that the heart of our agent remained untouched even when SDK APIs evolved.

We then demonstrated the power of this isolation by integrating our stable core with the OpenAI Agents SDK, showing how familiar tasks, like producing structured JSON and invoking tools, executed without any changes to the agent's core definitions. Finally, we built a ***second runtime adapter*** for an alternative SDK and showed how to plug it into the same core logic, proving that only the runtime layer changed.

CHAPTER 7: AGENT PACKAGING AND DEPLOYMENT

Overview

In this chapter, we will shift our focus from building the internal mechanics of the agent to packaging and deploying it like a small product. You will learn how to transform the working agent into a structured CLI tool with proper commands and runtime flags, allowing us to switch models and endpoints directly from the command line. We will then expose the same core logic through a minimal HTTP API that returns validated structured JSON, enabling other services to integrate with the agent safely and predictably. Throughout the chapter, we will maintain architectural discipline by ensuring that packaging layers wrap the core without modifying it.

Next, we will containerize the entire application into a single Docker image that can operate in either CLI or API mode depending on environment variables. You will see how configuration-driven design makes deployments consistent and portable across environments. Finally, we will consolidate the project into a reusable starter template repository snapshot, complete with clean structure, environment documentation, and versioning. By the end of this chapter, we will understand how to ship the agent as a small, maintainable product ready for reuse and deployment.

Three Packaging Paths

Up to this point, we did focus on architecture, structured outputs, tool contracts, model switching, SDK adapters, and local inference. So far, the agent works well. It can call tools. It can validate structured JSON. It can switch models and runtimes without rewrites.

Now we shift from building an agent to ***shipping it like a small product***.

If an agent only runs from a Python script on the laptop, it's a prototype. An agent that can be run from the command line, exposed as an HTTP service, and deployed in a container is a product artifact. The packaging is like the bridge between coming up with new ideas and making them easy to use.

So here, there are three practical packaging paths that cover nearly all real-world use cases:

1. ***CLI Application*** for developers, automation, and scripting.
2. ***HTTP API Service*** for integration with other systems. And,
3. ***Docker Container*** for reproducible deployment anywhere.

And, all these three together allow us to run the agent locally, integrate it into larger systems, and deploy it consistently across environments.

CLI Application as Packaging Path

A CLI interface turns the agent into something executable like this:

```
python -m agent_app "summarize: explain structured outputs"
```

Now here, why is the CLI packaging so important? I will tell you why. It really helps quick experimentation, supports shell scripting and automation, allows integration into CI pipelines, and makes regression testing straightforward.

While considering the CLI app as the packaing, we do not have to write the ad-hoc scripts repeatedly. Instead, we can formalize a reusable CLI entrypoint.

In the following, I will show you to create packaging artifact for our project. We will simply copy the following in the newly created file **src/cli.py**:

```
# src/cli.py
import sys
from src.agent_core.orchestrator import run_agent
from src.agent_core.schemas import AgentOutput
def main():
    if len(sys.argv) < 2:
        print("Usage: python -m src.cli \"your prompt here\"")
        sys.exit(1)
    prompt = sys.argv[1]
    raw_output = run_agent(prompt)
    validated = AgentOutput.parse_raw(raw_output)
    print(validated.json(indent=2))
if __name__ == "__main__":
    main()
```

Then, we will test it:

```
python -m src.cli "calculate: 5 * 8"
```

Once we do it, we now have a reusable CLI artifact. There is no architecture changed, and the CLI simply calls the core easily.

HTTP API Service as Packaging Path

Although the CLI is useful for developers, but the real systems communicate over HTTP. So here, if another service wants to call the agent, it cannot execute a CLI command. It needs an API endpoint.

So here, we will create a minimal HTTP wrapper using FastAPI as shown below:

```
POST /run
src/api.py
```

And, now we implement:

```
# src/api.py
from fastapi import FastAPI
from pydantic import BaseModel
from src.agent_core.orchestrator import run_agent
from src.agent_core.schemas import AgentOutput
app = FastAPI()
class AgentRequest(BaseModel):
   prompt: str
@app.post("/run", response_model=AgentOutput)
def run(request: AgentRequest):
   raw_output = run_agent(request.prompt)
   validated = AgentOutput.parse_raw(raw_output)
   return validated
```

After this, we then run the following:

```
uvicorn src.api:app --reload
```

And then, we will test as shown below:

```
curl -X POST http://localhost:8000/run \
 -H "Content-Type: application/json" \
 -d '{"prompt":"summarize: explain adapters"}'
```

Now in this packaging type, you will see that:

- We did not change the core,
- We reused the same orchestrator,

- We reused the same schema and,
- We reused the same validation logic.

In this packaging, the API layer is just a thin wrapper. This confirms our architectural discipline is working.

Docker Container as Packaging Path

The CLI works locally. And, the HTTP works on the machine. But the Docker makes the agent portable and reproducible, which has an edge on both the previous packaging methods.

So, in this, if someone else wants to run the agent, they should not manually install dependencies and not configure environments by trial and error.

Also, they should not care about the OS, as the docker solves that. In the following, we will learn the docker technique of packaging it:

To start with, we will first create a docker file in project root:

```
Dockerfile
```

And then, we will add the following:

```
FROM python:3.11-slim
WORKDIR /app
COPY requirements.txt .
RUN pip install --no-cache-dir -r requirements.txt
COPY . .
EXPOSE 8000
CMD ["uvicorn", "src.api:app", "--host", "0.0.0.0", "--port",
"8000"]
```

After this, we then build and run:

```
docker build -t agent-product .
docker run -p 8000:8000 agent-product
```

After running it, you will see that our agent is now:

- Containerized,
- Portable,

- Deployable to any cloud, and
- Ready for Kubernetes, ECS, or any container runtime.

In this packaging technique too, we did not touch the core.

All these three wraps or the packaging paths covers the same Agent App Core. And, it is not accidental. The core remains untouched.

The CLI supports:

- Testing,
- Batch jobs, and
- Internal automation.

The HTTP API supports:

- Web apps,
- Microservices,
- Mobile clients, and
- Internal tools.

And, the Docker supports:

- Cloud deployment,
- Versioned releases,
- Infrastructure automation, and
- Production rollout.

With all these above three paths, the agent is no longer a code experiment. It is now a product, although it is a small one but a product.

Translating Agent into CLI

In the previous topic, we learned to create a minimal CLI entry script and it was useful. But it was not yet product-grade. A real CLI must behave like a proper tool, and it should:

- Accept subcommands such as **`run`** and **`compare`**,
- Allow switching models without editing environment variables,
- Allow switching base URLs from the command line, and
- Reuse our existing core and adapters without modification.

The real goal here is not just convenience. The goal is ***portability***.

If we can switch models and endpoints from the command line without touching code, then we can say that,

- Our core is stable,
- Our gateway abstraction works,
- Our SDK adapters are runtime shells, and
- Our packaging layer is thin and clean.

In the following, we will now build a proper CLI interface.

Structured CLI Entry

For this build, we will prefer to use Python's built-in **argparse** module so we do not need to introduce unnecessary dependencies later.

To begin, we will first update our **src/cli.py** with the following code:

```
# src/cli.py
import argparse
import os
from src.agent_core.orchestrator import run_agent
from src.agent_core.schemas import AgentOutput
from compare_models import run_comparison
def main():
   parser = argparse.ArgumentParser(description="Agent CLI")
   subparsers = parser.add_subparsers(dest="command",
required=True)
   # run command
   run_parser = subparsers.add_parser("run", help="Run a
single prompt")
   run_parser.add_argument("--prompt", required=True)
   run_parser.add_argument("--model", required=False)
   run_parser.add_argument("--base-url", required=False)
   # compare command
   compare_parser = subparsers.add_parser("compare",
help="Compare models")
```

```
    compare_parser.add_argument("--model", action="append",
required=True)
    compare_parser.add_argument("--base-url", required=False)
    args = parser.parse_args()
    if args.base_url:
        os.environ["API_BASE_URL"] = args.base_url
    if args.model:
        if isinstance(args.model, list):
            os.environ["MODEL_NAME"] = args.model[0]
        else:
            os.environ["MODEL_NAME"] = args.model
    if args.command == "run":
        raw_output = run_agent(args.prompt)
        validated = AgentOutput.parse_raw(raw_output)
        print(validated.json(indent=2))
    elif args.command == "compare":
        os.environ["MODEL_NAME"] = args.model[0]
        run_comparison()
if __name__ == "__main__":
    main()
```

now from the above script, we introduced:

- A **`run`** command,
- A **`compare`** command,
- **`--model`** flag, and
- **`--base-url`** flag.

These flags override environment configuration dynamically, which means no **`.env`** editing, no code changes, no restarts beyond execution itself.

Running Agent from CLI

Next, we will now execute the following simple prompt.

```
python -m src.cli run \
 --prompt "summarize: explain structured outputs" \
 --model openai:gpt-5.2 \
 --base-url https://api.openai.com/v1
```

This uses:

- Hosted model,
- Hosted endpoint, and
- Same stable core.

After this, we will now switch to local vLLM. And we will do this without touching any code:

```
python -m src.cli run \
 --prompt "summarize: explain structured outputs" \
 --model local:meta-llama/Llama-3.1-8B-Instruct \
 --base-url http://localhost:8000/v1
```

In the above, if you observe closely, only the **-model**, and **--base-url** are changed. Otherwise, the orchestrator, the schema, the tools, and the SDK adapter did not change.

Comparing Models from CLI

And, now is the time to test the **compare** command.

```
python -m src.cli compare \
 --model openai:gpt-5.2 \
 --model local:meta-llama/Llama-3.1-8B-Instruct \
 --base-url http://localhost:8000/v1
```

After running the above command,

- The CLI sets environment variables dynamically.
- The compare runner executes the same prompt across models.
- Results are saved as JSON files.
- Structured validation is reused. And,
- The core remains untouched.

The CLI simply orchestrates execution. It does not contain business logic and that is deliberate.

In real systems, we rarely want to edit source files just to test a different model. You want runtime flexibility. The CLI gives instant switching, reproducibility, scriptability, and clear interface boundaries.

This is the true and real difference between a demo and a product-grade tool.

Exposing HTTP API

A CLI is excellent for developers and automation. However, most real systems do not execute command-line tools directly. Web apps, mobile apps, internal dashboards, and microservices all communicate over HTTP. If we want our agent to behave like a small product rather than a developer utility, we must expose it behind a clean API endpoint.

The important constraint here is architectural discipline. The API layer must:

- Call the existing core orchestrator.
- Validate the structured JSON using our schema.
- Return the validated object.
- Avoid embedding business logic inside the HTTP layer.

The HTTP layer is merely a transport wrapper. The core remains untouched.

Let us build this carefully.

Creating API Wrapper

We will first implement the minimal HTTP wrapper using FastAPI in file **src/api.py**:

```
# src/api.py
from fastapi import FastAPI, HTTPException
from pydantic import BaseModel
from src.agent_core.orchestrator import run_agent
from src.agent_core.schemas import AgentOutput
app = FastAPI(title="GenAI Agent API")
class AgentRequest(BaseModel):
   prompt: str
@app.post("/run", response_model=AgentOutput)
def run(request: AgentRequest):
```

```
    try:
        raw_output = run_agent(request.prompt)
        validated = AgentOutput.parse_raw(raw_output)
        return validated
    except Exception as exc:
        raise HTTPException(status_code=500, detail=str(exc))
```

In the above code:

- The **AgentRequest** defines the expected input.
- The **response_model=AgentOutput** ensures the response conforms to our structured schema.
- The endpoint calls **run_agent**, which belongs to the stable core.
- Validation happens before returning. And,
- Errors are converted into HTTP responses.

However, you also must bserve here that we did not import any SDK directly, did not change the orchestrator, did not duplicate schema logic, and did not embed business logic into the API.

The API is kept so thin.

Run API Server

After creating, we just need to simply run the following to start the server:

```
uvicorn src.api:app --reload
Uvicorn running on http://127.0.0.1:8000
```

The FastAPI will generate the documentation at **http://127.0.0.1:8000/docs**. Once done, we can then test the endpoint from the browser, or we can make use of **curl**.

Send Test Request

With the following script, we can easily test the API:

```
curl -X POST http://localhost:8000/run \
  -H "Content-Type: application/json" \
  -d '{"prompt":"summarize: explain structured outputs"}'
```

After running the above script, we should get a structured JSON response, which is similar to the following:

```
{
 "answer": "...",
 "steps": ["...", "..."],
 "confidence": 0.91
}
```

Now here, what matters is the JSON structure matches **`AgentOutput`**, the API enforces schema validation, the same core logic executed underneath, and the model switching still works via environment variables or CLI flags.

Model Switching

While the API is running, we can also switch the models. For this, you run the following in a separate terminal:

```
export MODEL_NAME="local:meta-llama/Llama-3.1-8B-Instruct"
export API_BASE_URL="http://localhost:8000/v1"
```

After this, we just need to restart the API server and send the same HTTP request again. Overall, the API wrapper added zero new business logic, and that is the key success signal.

Dockerize CLI and API

Until now, we have two entry points i.e. a CLI interface (**`src.cli`**), and an HTTP API (**`src.api`**). Hence, instead of creating separate containers for each mode, we will create ***one Docker image*** that can run in either CLI mode or API mode depending on how it is started. And, this will give us:

- A single build artifact
- Reproducible deployments
- Environment-driven configuration
- Clean separation between code and runtime behavior

We will now begin.

Confirming Environment-driven Config

Before we begin to write the Dockerfile, we will first confirm that the configuration module reads values from environment variables.

For your ease, the **config.py** should look like the following:

```
# src/config.py
import os
MODEL_NAME = os.getenv("MODEL_NAME", "openai:gpt-5.2")
API_BASE_URL = os.getenv("API_BASE_URL",
"https://api.openai.com/v1")
API_KEY = os.getenv("API_KEY", "")
```

This step is important, as we do not hardcode models or the endpoints or the secrets. Everything is injected at runtime, and all such thing is making the container portable.

Creating Unified Entry

We will create a small launcher script that chooses between CLI and API modes in **src/entrypoint.py**:

```
# src/entrypoint.py
import os
import sys
import subprocess
MODE = os.getenv("APP_MODE", "api")
if MODE == "cli":
   # Forward CLI arguments
   subprocess.run(["python", "-m", "src.cli"] + sys.argv[1:])
else:
   # Default: run API server
   subprocess.run([
       "uvicorn",
       "src.api:app",
       "--host", "0.0.0.0",
       "--port", "8000"
```

```
])
```

After this, the behavior depends on:

```
APP_MODE=cli
```

or

```
APP_MODE=api
```

While doing this, the code modifications are not at all required.

Creating Dockerfile

Following Dockerfile is what we will create in the project root:

```
FROM python:3.11-slim
WORKDIR /app
COPY requirements.txt .
RUN pip install --no-cache-dir -r requirements.txt
COPY . .
ENV PYTHONUNBUFFERED=1
ENV APP_MODE=api
EXPOSE 8000
CMD ["python", "-m", "src.entrypoint"]
```

In the dockerfile,

- We install dependencies once.
- We copy the full project.
- We set default mode to API.
- We expose port 8000. And,
- We use a single entrypoint.

So basically, we create one image, but with two behaviors.

Building Docker Image

From project root, we will run the following

```
docker build -t genai-agent-product .
```

With this, we now have a reusable image.

Running API Mode

By default, the mode is API. We will run as shown below:

```
docker run -p 8000:8000 \
 -e MODEL_NAME="openai:gpt-5.2" \
 -e API_BASE_URL="https://api.openai.com/v1" \
 -e API_KEY="your-key" \
 genai-agent-product
```

And then, we can test:

```
curl -X POST http://localhost:8000/run \
 -H "Content-Type: application/json" \
 -d '{"prompt":"summarize: explain portability"}'
```

Once we are sure, that the API works, we then switch the models.

And to switch, we will first stop the container and run the following:

```
docker run -p 8000:8000 \
 -e MODEL_NAME="local:meta-llama/Llama-3.1-8B-Instruct" \
 -e API_BASE_URL="http://host.docker.internal:8000/v1" \
 -e API_KEY="local-key" \
 genai-agent-product
```

Here, the image did not change, only the environment variables gets changed.

Running CLI Mode

Now for this, we will use the same image in CLI mode.

```
docker run \
 -e APP_MODE=cli \
```

```
-e MODEL_NAME="openai:gpt-5.2" \
-e API_BASE_URL="https://api.openai.com/v1" \
-e API_KEY="your-key" \
genai-agent-product run \
--prompt "calculate: 9 * 9"
```

After running this, the container executed the CLI path, same image but different runtime behavior. And there is no code change at all.

After all this, the agent is no longer a script. It is just a deployable unit.

Shipping "Starter Template" Repo

Up to this point, we built:

- A stable Agent App Core,
- Runtime adapters,
- Model gateway abstraction,
- CLI packaging,
- HTTP API wrapper, and
- Docker container

And, all this is a working product.

However, a real product is a code that can be reused, cloned, extended, and adapted quickly. Hence, in this topic, we will learn our final step, which is to convert our project into a ***starter template repository snapshot*** that others can fork and immediately begin building upon.

To give you a quick understanding, a starter template is basically:

- Minimal,
- Stable but extensible,
- Config-driven,
- Cleanly structured, and
- Free of environment-specific artifacts.

So now, we will learn to finalize the project:

Cleaning Project Structure

You need to ensure that the final structure of our project looks something like this:

```
genai-agent-template/
├── src/
│   ├── agent_core/
│   │   ├── orchestrator.py
│   │   ├── tools.py
│   │   └── schemas.py
│   │       └── prompts.py
│   ├── model_gateway.py
│   ├── openai_sdk_adapter.py
│   ├── other_sdk_adapter.py
│   ├── cli.py
│   ├── api.py
│   ├── entrypoint.py
│   └── config.py
├── compare_models.py
├── requirements.txt
├── Dockerfile
├── README.md
├── .env.example
└── .gitignore
```

Each file you see above exists for a reason. And, there is:

- Clear separation of core and runtime,
- Clear packaging boundaries,
- No SDK logic inside core, and
- No hardcoded secrets.

Creating .env example file

A template must guide users without exposing secrets. So here, we will create:

```
.env.example
```

And then, within this file, we will add:

```
MODEL_NAME=openai:gpt-5.2
API_BASE_URL=https://api.openai.com/v1
API_KEY=your-api-key-here
APP_MODE=api
```

This file records the required environment variables. It does not contain real credentials. Thereby, you may consider the template very much safe and professional.

Creating README

We will now. Create the **`README.md`** as shown below:

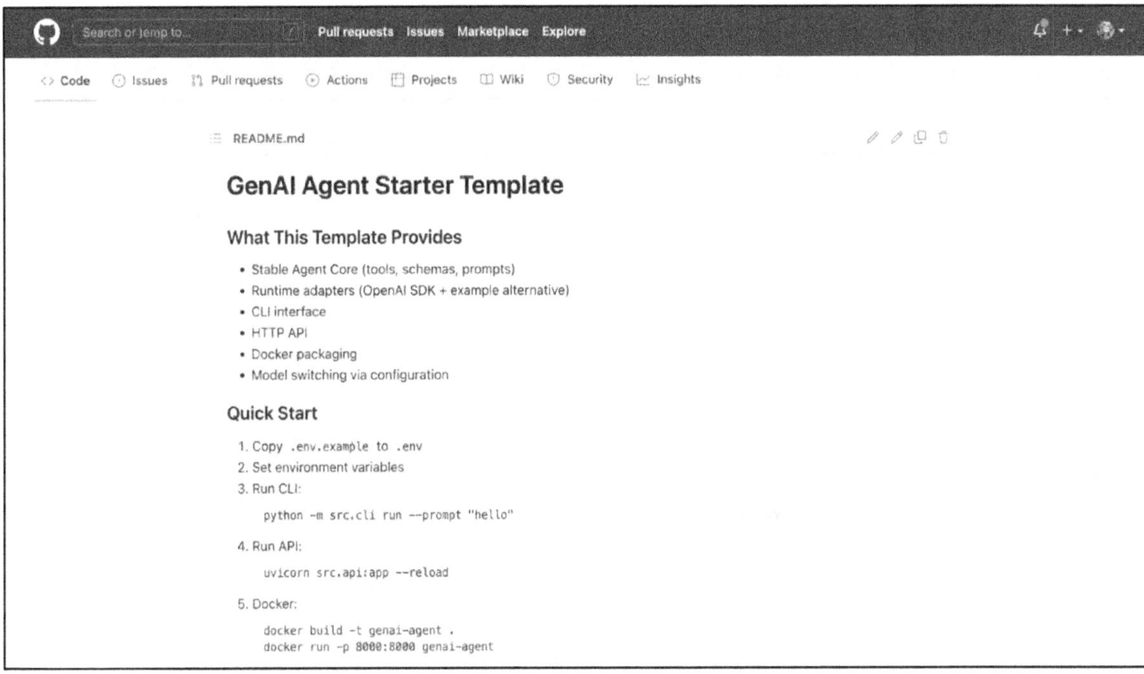

Fig 7.1 README Template

We will keep it short, clear, and actionable.

Removing Non-Template Artifacts

Now, before we do the snapshotting of the the repo, we will:

- Remove local test outputs,
- Remove generated comparison JSON files,
- Remove **`.pyc`** files, and
- Remove model cache directories.

We also need to ensure that the **`.gitignore`** includes the following:

```
__pycache__/
.env
```

```
model_comparison_outputs/
*.log
```

This is needed to be done such that the starter template remains clean.

Adding Version Metadata

We can then add a simple version file:

```
VERSION
```

And its content would be very simple:

```
0.1.0
```

This small addition signals that the template is versioned. If someone extends it, they can increment the version. This turns the repo into a product artifact rather than a loose collection of files.

Tagging Snapshot

Now to tag, we can git the following:

```
git add .
git commit -m "Initial starter template snapshot"
git tag v0.1.0
```

With the above, the repository is snapshot-stable, clone-ready, and extensible. After doing all this, a developer can:

- Add new tools to **`agent_core/tools.py`**,
- Add new schemas to **`schemas.py`**,
- Add a new SDK adapter,
- Change models without rewriting,
- Deploy locally or to cloud,
- Extend CLI commands,
- Add authentication to API, and
- Integrate into larger systems

And, all this we or you can do without disturbing the architectural foundation.

Project Quick Revisit

To quickly summarize, what this entire book has taught in series, is that, we first started with a simple loop-based agent.

And then, we progressively added:

- Structured outputs,
- Tool contracts,
- Validation and regression tests,
- Model gateway abstraction,
- Local vLLM support,
- SDK runtime adapters,
- CLI packaging,
- HTTP API exposure,
- Docker deployment, and
- Template snapshotting

After all this, we can proudly say that we have built an agent which is ***portable, swappable, structured, and a true deployable system***. The core principle that carried us through every chapter is stable business logic, swappable runtimes, and configuration-driven flexibility.

With this, you are all set to to build production-grade GenAI agents without architectural rewrites., and well trained too, to ship agents across any packaging method.

Summary

Overall, we moved from a working agent to a packaged, deployable product in this chapter. We created a proper CLI with structured commands such as run and compare, allowed model names and base URLs to be switched directly from the command line. We then wrapped the same stable core behind a minimal HTTP API that returned validated JSON responses, ensuring that structured schemas remained enforced even in networked environments. Throughout this process, we avoided embedding business logic inside the CLI or API layers. We also reinforced the idea that runtime flexibility comes from configuration, and not from rewriting application code.

Later, we containerized the agent into a single Docker image capable of running in either CLI or API mode based on environment variables. We demonstrated how environment-driven configuration keeps deployments portable and consistent across machines and environments. Finally, we finalized the project into a reusable starter template repository snapshot with clean structure, versioning, and documented configuration. By the end of the chapter, we had converted our agent into a portable, reproducible, and extensible small product without altering the stable core logic.

Index

S

T

V

Epilogue

These days, AI agents are moving from experimental prototypes to everyday software components. More and more, businesses are checking out how agents can help with their internal workflows, automate repetitive analysis, and support decision-making processes. At the same time, people are discovering how small agents can make personal tasks like organizing information, summarizing documents, or interacting with digital services easier. It might seem like a lot is happening all at once, but it's actually a step-by-step process. A lot of organizations are still figuring out how to integrate these systems safely and effectively into their existing processes. The move from experimental tools to reliable infrastructure will take time, and it'll depend a lot on smart engineering practices. A big thing that'll happen in the next few years is agents becoming more like modular systems instead of one-size-fits-all apps. A lot of the time, early implementations combined models, prompts, tools, and infrastructure in a single application that was closely linked. As the ecosystem matures, the developers are separating these components more and more so that each part can evolve on its own. Even if models improve, inference engines get faster, and SDKs keep changing, the logic that defines what an agent does can stay the same. This separation lets organizations try out new technologies without having to rebuild their apps all the time.

In places where there are already well-defined workflows, businesses are more likely to start using agents. There are a few areas where you could start, like customer support, finding info within the company, and data analysis. In these situations, agents can help people instead of taking their place. They can help teams deal with a lot of information or automate repetitive steps in a process. With time, organizations can start to use these agents in more complex scenarios. Having said that, it's going to take a lot of people using it for it to be a thing. And if the systems that you use produce structured outputs, follow clear tool contracts, and integrate smoothly with existing software, they'll be easier to trust and maintain. In general, people will come across AI agents in different ways. Some interactions will happen through familiar interfaces like messaging apps, productivity tools, or search platforms. Others will be working behind the scenes, helping out with things like organizing schedules, summarizing long documents, or interacting with digital services. For a lot of people, these agents won't seem like a huge change, but more like a slow improvement in how well software systems work and how useful they are.

The most important lesson we can learn is that building AI agents is about more than just intelligence. Structure and discipline are also super important. The tech behind large language models is going to keep changing really fast. There'll be new inference engines, more model capabilities, and different development frameworks. It's good to have clear boundaries between core logic and runtime components in your systems, so you'll be more prepared to adapt. If you rely too much on one framework or provider, you might find yourself rebuilding systems more often than you'd like.

Basically, if this book has done its part, that means creating AI agents doesn't need fancy structures or weak connections. A well-structured agent can start out as a small Python program and gradually grow into a deployable application with a CLI, an HTTP API, and a containerized deployment. Even better, that agent can keep up with the latest tech changes. As AI agents become more common in business and everyday software, it'll become really important to be able to build them in a way that's durable and easy to move around.

Thank You